REVENUE
STAMP

THE
REVENUE
STAMP

An Autobiography

AMRITA PRITAM

Translated by
Krishna Gorowara

An Imprint of **Vikas Publishing House Pvt Ltd**
E-28, Sector-8, Noida-201301 (UP) India
Phone: +91-120-4078900, Fax: +91-120-4078999
E-mail: helpline@vikaspublishing.com • www.vikaspublishing.com

First Published in 1994

Reprinted edition 2016

Copyright © Amrita Pritam

All rights reserved

ISBN 978-93-259-9134-7

Marketed and Distributed exclusively in India & subcontinent by:

Times Group Books
(A division of Bennett, Coleman and Co. Ltd.)
Times Annexe, Express Building
9-10, Bahadur Shah Zafar Marg, New Delhi-110 002

Printed in India

Contents

1

RESURRECTING TIME

Is it Doomsday?

Moments of my life in the womb of time—lived awhile, and after Time's span, seemingly entombed—are today alive again, stalk past me . . .

How have all the graves yielded to resurrect those moments? It must indeed be Doomsday . . .

This is an aubade from a 1918 grave, a year before I was born. It comes to me now for the first time: so far I had only heard about it.

Both my parents were teachers at Panih Khand Bhassaur School. The two daughters of Babu Teja Singh, the founder of the school, were among their pupils. What inspired them one day, I would not know, but both organized a *kirtan* in the Gurudwara, said their prayers, and wound up with a special one for the occasion: 'Hearken to these voices, O Lord, please grant the boon of a child to our teacher . . .'

When my father, who was in the congregation, heard these words he flared up at my mother. He suspected that the special prayer was my mother's doing. She, poor soul, was as surprised as he was. Babu Teja Singh's daughters explained later that if they had taken my mother Raj Bibi into confidence, she might have asked for the birth of a son. But they wanted a girl in their master's house—a girl like themselves.

Why did those girls think of this very strange prayer? I don't know. But the prayer was heard. Within a year from that day, Raj Bibi had become a mother.

Just as amazingly, a moment from ten years earlier, wakes up from the womb of Time—the moment when Raj Bibi, only twenty years of age, offered her homage at the habitation of *sadhus* at Gujranwala, and there saw Nand Sadhu . . .

Nand Sadhu was the son of a wealthy moneylender. When he was only six months old, his mother Lachmi died. His maternal grandmother wrapped him up in her arms and got a grain-winnower as wet-nurse.

Nand had four brothers and a sister—but two of his brothers had died; one—Gopal Singh—an inveterate drunkard, forsook his family for the love of the bottle; the other—Hakim Singh—took to the life of a *sadhu*. So Nand knew only his elder sister, Hakko, whom he grew to love dearly.

From all I have heard, she was a bewitching creature and was married when she came of age. But the moment she saw her groom, Bela Singh, she knew he was not the one for her. On her first visit to her parental home after her marriage, she asked for a basement to be built. As soon as it was ready, she betook herself to it and fasted for forty days. She then took the saffron robes and lived on cooked grams soaked overnight in plain water. Nand followed suit. He also began to wear saffron robes. Alas! His sister did not live long and when she died, Nand renounced the world.

He turned his back on the incalculable wealth his grandfather, Amar Singh Sachdev, the moneylender, had left him, and went and joined Sant Dayal's *ashram*. There he learnt Sanskrit, Braj *bhasha* and the lore of *hakims*. They used to call him Bal Sadhu—the young holiness.

While his sister was still alive, Nand's aunt and uncle had him betrothed to a girl in Amritsar. Nand broke off the engagement and began writing poems steeped in the spirit of renunciation.

Raj Bibi was from the village Monga in Gujarat district, and was married through the prevalent barter system. But the man to whom her life was to be linked went and got himself recruited as a soldier. No one heard of him again. For Raj Bibi it was a life without hope, an empty life. But what matters is not life but the courage you bring to it. She began teaching in a school at Gujranwala. Every day on her way to school, she would first go with her sister-in-law to Dayalji's *ashram* for her prayers. Her brother had died. Her widowed sister-in-law's brother had been exchanged with hers for a husband. But now, the two lost souls taught in the same school and kept house together. One day, when Raj Bibi and her sister-in-law were at Dayalji's *ashram,* it started raining heavily. There was no question of anyone leaving the *ashram* in that rain. So Dayalji asked Bal Sadhu to recite some poems till the weather cleared. Bal Sadhu was in the habit of closing his eyes as he recited. The recital over, he opened them and they were immediately attracted towards Raj Bibi and could not take them off her. Dayalji noticed this. He did not say anything immediately but some days later took Nand aside and said: 'Nand, my boy, this life of renunciation is not for you. Give up these saffron robes and get married.'

That was how Raj Bibi became my mother, and Nand Sadhu my father. On his marriage, Nand changed his name to Kartar Singh. Since he wrote poetry, he had also taken on a pseudonym—*Peeyookh*—the Sanskrit word for nectar. Ten years later when I was born, he named me 'Amrita', the Punjabi equivalent for *peeyookh;* while he himself changed his *nom de plume* to Hitkari.

The most remarkable thing about father was that a life of riches or renunciation came alike to him. Mother used to relate a story about a brother *sadhu*, another disciple of Dayalji, Sant Harnam Singh by name, whose elder brother wanted to marry. A girl had been bespoken, but because he had no house, the question of marriage was ruled out. My father had one house, still left from his inheritance. He said: 'If it's only for want of a house that he can't get married, I'll transfer mine in his name.' And so it was. Then for the rest of his life my father lived in rented places. He could never build another house of his own; yet I do not remember ever having seen or heard any sign of regret from him.

What I do remember is a regret of another sort, transfixed in his expression after mother died, when I was only ten years of age. He again sought renunciation. I was the only bondage in his world. Love for me and a desire for complete withdrawal were the two conflicting forces that tormented him. I sensed all this and used to cry out in anguish because I could not tell whether I was accepted or not. I was both accepted and rejected in turn.

Having taught me all he could about rhyme and rhythm, my father's desire was that I should find expression in poetry. I began writing and it seems to me I wrote because I wanted to forget those moments of rejection I felt in him.

Half a century later, I feel that both riches and renunciation have taken twin birth in me as well. This I have inherited, like my features, I think, from Father. Perhaps I see things with the same eyes that he did . . .

Only, I keep wondering if I have accepted myself for what I am. That is why perhaps I have written all my life—so that whatever I could not accept in me, I would in time not reject altogether.

I did not then think of the world or of what the world thought of me. My only desire was to please Father. It is the same now. I am not in the least mindful of what others think of me. My only desire is to be at peace with my innermost self.

I never told an untruth to Father; I can never lie to myself either.

This brings me to Grandmother, who reigned supreme in the kitchen, if not in the house. My father's revolt was against her regime. I used to notice three glass tumblers kept away from all other pots and pans on a shelf in the corner of the kitchen. These were for use only when Father's Muslim friends were offered tea or buttermilk when they came to visit him. After these tumblers had served their purpose, they were scrubbed and washed and put right back in their ostracized niche.

The three tumblers became a 'cause' for me, and the four of us put up a fight with Grandmother. I was adamant; I would not drink from any other tumbler but one of those. Grandmother would rather see me thirsty than let me use them. The tale, inevitably, travelled to Father. He, of course, did not until then have the faintest idea about such things. The moment he did, I succeeded in my revolt. Thereafter, not a single utensil was labelled 'Hindu' or 'Muslim'.

Neither Grandmother nor I knew then that the man I was to fall in love with would be of the same faith as the branded utensils were meant for.

Young as I was, I wonder whether the shadow of my fate had not so been cast on me already.

Shadows have a reality longer than is recognized. Faces too have a reality. But for how long? Shadows for as long as you like. For a lifetime, if you will.

Years come and go. They do not wait. Some shadows, on the other hand, hover around us with an existence of their own.

Shadows are related to entities; they are subservient to entities. Yet some do not fit into any such pattern.

Sometimes it seems as if a shadow is cast on you from nowhere. Broken away, it falls in your path, and you have to carry it along with you to whichever part of the world you go—in search of the entity from which it broke off.

Illusions too can be cast over your mind. You measure a particular shadow to the length of a stranger—and see if it fits.

If it does not, so what? You take the shadow along and move on.

There was one such shadow in my life. Does one name a shadow? I, anyway, named it 'Rajan'.

There was a tradition in the family. We said a prayer, *Kirtan Sohela,* before retiring for the night. Father believed that with each syllable of the prayer, faith itself got fortified. And as the prayer ended, you stood as some sentinel of a fort which was secure from all sides, allowing no entry. And free from all anxieties and worries, you fell into the sleep of the just.

But, reciting the prayer before going to bed, when we were drowsy, with eyes heavy, it could happen that half the prayer was left unsaid even though Father maintained that it had to be said to the very last word. Should the tiniest bit be left out, the Fort became vulnerable.

I was a child then. I was worried for the complete security of the Fort. How would Rajan come into my dreams? Whilst I was inside the Fort, he might be left out! So I would decide to mumble some lines from memory and deliberately leave out a few while tumbling and tossing in my bed. By this ruse, the Fort would not be so firmly held and he could enter from the gaps purposely left open.

But Father changed the ritual a little. Instead of each of us saying the prayer separately in our individual beds, he decided to say it aloud from his bed for us all to sit up and hear. This change was perhaps because we then had some distant relatives who had come to stay with us, a boy and a girl, and also perhaps because the little girl was finding it difficult to memorize some parts of the prayer. In that way no line would be omitted. Once or twice, I tried some skipping. Father instantly saw to it that the lapse was corrected. So there was no getting away with my pranks. Yet, after a good deal of effort, I saw a way out. What if Rajan were called in before prayer began? So, before the Fort closed on all sides, he could be by my side.

I was ten then. Forty years later, now when I think of that prank of mine, it seems that whatever I have wanted with all my heart, I have found. Around me, forts have been raised and demolished but the reality of the One, has in one form or the other, always been with me. At one time in the features and form of a man's face; at another in what has taken shape from my pen; and at yet another some sort of divinity has arisen from the leaves of a book or has stepped out from a canvas to be with me. Like a genie from a streak of smoke it emerges—sometimes from the anguish that goes into the making of a song, from the budding leaf of a twig, even from the moon as it shines on the waves of the sea. At times, when I am engulfed in my loneliness, I have found it gushing forth—coursing in the veins and speeding up the flow of blood in my body. And with all this, the pallor that should otherwise come with weariness of a kind, takes on a fresh colour.

If pervades all my thoughts and dreams to such a degree that even fleeting goodness seems to be a manifestation of that One. And it is so beautiful that I cry . . .

Abstractions have no meaning for me. Each entity must take on some sort of shape or form; that I can touch, that in fact, can thrill me with a touch.

In the years of my nonage, whenever I dreamt of the *Gurus*—Har Gobind or more often of Gobind Singh—I always ran my fingertips over the portrait; the horse he rode on, the sword he carried, the falcon he held in his hand, anything. I would never pay homage from a distance. If in a slightly different way, flowers or leafy boughs too I hold to myself as in embrace. My entire being is filled with such a sense of belonging as to make my very breath heavy.

Many, many years ago, the One sat by my side. He had a soiled handkerchief. I took it away, giving him a clean one. His, I kept for years. My forehead burned with a yearning whenever I touched it.

There are certain seeds that once fertilized in the soil, can survive without leaf and branch, no matter how furious the tempest, how searing the hot wind of drought. They just cannot be uprooted. In the same way is the longing for the One, and respect for the Word. Such seeds indeed sprouted in my womb in the prime of my life, but faith was shattered utterly. I feel both these trees should have been uprooted. Sometimes deep down I have a feeling that they no longer exist. But from the dry dusts of the mind, they sprout forth again and become sturdy branches; branches strong enough to blossom and bear fruit. And with the breath of my life, I receive their fragrance.

One seed I sowed myself; for the other, Father was responsible. Should a page from a book be found on the floor, he would pick it up with solemn respect. Should my foot by chance fall on it, he would be angry. Thus has been deeply engrained in my mind, respect for the written word—and with that for all those who wield the pen. That was how I came to look up to Bhai Sahib Kahan Singh, Father's friend. The very threshold of our house seemed benigned when he entered. A portrait of Father's Guru, Dayalji, that rare scholar of Sanskrit, hung at the head of Father's bed. Even to sit with feet stretched out in the direction of that portrait was forbidden.

So when I grew up, I had the utmost respect for my contemporaries. But my sad experiences with them leave me wondering why this respect for the word and the pen has not vanished long ago.

Sometimes I wonder whether my contemporaries are the only ones with whom I have dealt.

Beyond time and distance, perhaps, are so many like Kazantzakis, so many who have watered this tree. Why then do I wonder if this tree is still green?

July 31, 1930

I was hardly eleven when Mother suddenly fell ill. Barely a week later, with pale, drawn faces, friends and relatives assembled at her bedside.

'Where's my Binna?' She had asked. By the time her friend Pritam Kaur had led me by the hand to her, she had lost consciousness.

'Pray to God . . . maybe He'll show mercy . . . a child's prayers never go unheeded . . .' the good lady said to me.

My feet were glued to the spot where I stood. I had from my early days learnt the art of disciplined meditation. Now when occasion called, it was an easy enough exercise. I had just to close my eyes and fold my hands for the simple prayer: 'Please don't let Mother die.'

My mother bore her illness calmly. There was no wail of agony from her. But there was a general bewilderment among those around. 'Why are they losing their nerves?' I asked myself. 'Mother's anguish is over. I am imploring Him . . . He listens to what children say . . .'

My mother lay there in all serenity. Suddenly I knew it was the end. Everyone wept and wailed. I burst out in red hot rage, 'God heeds no one, not even children . . .'

From that day, I gave up all the meditation and prayer I had been brought up with over the years. Father did not approve. He became stricter, but I was vehement in my resistance:

'There is no God.'

'You mustn't say that.'

'Why not?'

'He has ways of showing His wrath . . .'

'Let Him! But how can He when He isn't there . . .?'

'How do you know?'

'Wouldn't He have heard me . . . had He been anywhere?'

'What did you say to Him?'

'I said: "Please don't let Mother die".'

'When did you see Him? He cannot be seen . . .'

'But can't He hear? Is He deaf?'

During routine prayers, Father firmly stood his ground. I, as firmly, stood mine. Unable to hold back his anger, he would sometimes take me by the shoulders and force me down cross-legged to pray, with the command, 'Close your eyes! Concentrate for ten minutes!'

When I could not resist his authority any longer, I would sit down cross-legged and close my eyes. But giving in to physical defeat only made me seethe with anger inside. 'I've closed my eyes, what can He do to me if I don't concentrate? I refuse to have anything to do with a God who has not heard me. I refuse to dwell on what His image looks like. I'll bring Rajan to my mind instead. He dallies with me in my dreams; he hears my songs; he makes such lovely pictures of me . . . That's it . . .! I'll fix my mind on Rajan!'

For years I dreamt those dreams I held so dear. Summer and winter, my dreams became a steady ritual with me.

I dreamt of a great big dark castle, with my little self a prisoner within. Armed guards stood without. I looked in vain for a door that would open at my touch. In the murkiness overwhelming me, I groped about, but the strong walls of rock would not melt or fade away. Helpless, I tried in vain to fly up and over. I flapped and fluttered my arms till I fell down breathless. And then . . . slowly and softly, I felt my feet rising above the ground . . . higher and yet higher, up above the turrets and towers to hail the blue expanse of the sky! Fearless, I flew over the vast expanse of the earth below . . . the guards flailing their arms but failing to reach out and catch me.

Another dream which lived with me for years was of a crowd of people in wild pursuit . . . with me fleeing them. The chase would go on and on . . . as the crowd would draw near, my anxiety would increase and I would run faster till I sighted a river. My pursuers would be wildly jubilant: 'Where'll she go now? There's the river ahead!' Seeing no way out, I'd then calmly walk across over the water. The flow of the river would take on a strange solidity, and give support to my feet. The cooling limpidity of the water was to my mind better than the hard ground which sometimes gave me blisters on my feet... The crowd would come to a dead stop. No one would dare to step into the water for fear of being drowned. They would stand on the bank and scowl and growl and clench and thrust their fists out . . . But I had escaped them all . . .

My Sixteenth Year

Came my sixteenth year—like a stranger. Inside me, there was an awareness I could not explain.

Except for Father, there was no one else in our house. He wrote away and sometimes would keep at his work all through the night and sleep during the day. Had Mother been alive, my sixteenth year would have been different; it would have come like a friend, a near relative . . . But without Mother, there was a great deal missing from my life. To shield me from outside influences, Father thought it right that I should have no familiarity with anyone: not with any girl from school nor with any boy from the neighbourhood.

Like a thief, came my sixteenth year, stealthily like a prowler in the night, stealing in through the open window at the head of my bed . . .

Our house was full of books. Most of them were on religion, about *rishis* and about meditation. There were a few books of history but into these too, *apsaras* sometimes intruded—like Menaka or Urvashi, out to seduce the meditating *rishis*. It was reading them that my sixteenth year broke through the age of my innocence . . .

Every *apsara* disturbing the meditations of a *rishi* was, mythologically speaking, the commissary of Lord Indra. My sixteenth year must also have been Lord Indra's work, invading the purity of my childhood. It was now that I began to write poetry, and on every poem I wrote, I carried the cross of forbidden desires. Just as the *rishis* became restless as each *apsara* appeared, so my rebellious thoughts pursued me, giving me no peace . . .

And yet that year established no kinship with me. It was a clandestine relationship. Like me, it was scared of Father. As it stood away from me behind a door, every poem I wrote I tore to bits and appeared before Father, an innocent, dutiful child.

Not that he objected to my writing poetry. He had himself given me my first lessons in metrical composition. But what he expected from me was religious verse, orthodox and conventional in style.

That was how my sixteenth year came and went. Nothing very significant happened. Yet life took on a different meaning. It was the beginning of the uneven road of life with all its hairpin bends, its ups and downs. It was also the beginning of curiosity. I questioned parental authority; I questioned the

value of doing my work at school by rote; I questioned what
had been preached to me and I questioned the entire stratified
social scheme. What I had so far learnt was like a straitjacket
that gives way at the seams—as the body grows. I was thirsty
for life. I wanted living contact with those stars I had been
taught to worship from afar. What I got instead was advice and
constraint which only fed my rebellion.

I suppose everyone goes through this phase. But it
happened to me with three times greater impact. First, there
was the drabness of middle-class morality; then the dosage of
'don'ts' thrust down my throat which I somehow felt I would
have been spared had my mother been alive. There was the
overbearing presence of my father, a man of religion. Poor
Father. He wanted me to be an obedient, self-effacing daughter
and here was I in my sixteenth year bearing my cross like the
pang of an unfulfilled love. I was sixteen and the memory creeps
into every phase of my life . . .

I caught its spirit again and again. At the time of the
partition of the country in 1947, when all social, political and
religious values came crashing down like glass smashed into
smithereens under the feet of people in flight . . . Those crushed
pieces of glass bruised my soul and my limbs bled. I wrote
my hymns for the suffering of those who were abducted and
raped. The passion of those monstrous times has been with
me since, like some consuming fire—when I wrote later of a
beloved's face; of the aggressors from neighbouring countries;
of the crime of the long Vietnamese night, or, at one stage, of

the helpless Czechs . . . In the haunting image of beauty and in the anger at wrong and cruelty, my sixteenth year stretches on and on . . .

I thank the fates that conspired to break through the years of my innocence. That conspiracy relates not only to that one year alone but to the whole of my life.

Each thought of mine year after year, intrudes upon those innocent years. I pity the patience and resignation of those who come to terms with wrong. I am happy I have not had the solace of peace as I go alone on my restless quest . . . except, perhaps, that I have acquired since, the sense to discern. And like in my sixteenth year, I do not negotiate my wails by stealth. I do not avoid confrontation. As I begin my fiftieth year, my feelings have the same intensity. Even now, everything around me seems to constrict the soul just as the clothes one grows out of during adolescence. The lips are parched with the thirst for life; desire comes back to stretch the hand and touch the stars. Wherever in the world a wrong is done, I continue to feel a deep sense of outrage.

A Shadow

A deep dark shadow walked along my side for as long as I can remember. It gradually came on me that much was layered into it: the face of my ideal lover, and mine, that I imagined growing wiser, stronger, more mature. The layer deepest down was of the freedom of my own and other lands.

Whatever I wrote was inspired by this shadow, to which I gave flesh and blood, a vague mass in which I sought to reveal something luminous in quality.

Was this out of a longing to embody God—a God with so many faces? The moments of my life expand to reveal beauteous concepts and forms . . . Those moments were painful, like the bird song in the morning, heard one moment, lost the next. I remember writing once, 'I have many contemporaries, only I am not contemporaneous.'

It was well if someone gave ear to my songs. I had no right to claim it.

I was yet a child when I heard those myriad voices of hate and abuse. There were flags of so many denominations and so many flagstaffs on which they fluttered. They thought I too wanted to fly one of my own. I wanted to cry out to them all, 'My friends, have no illusions. You're welcome to your faiths and your flags. I want nothing.' But did anyone care? Would a time come when they would hear? Not when it came to my own language. This is as true today as it was thirty years ago.

This was my first painful experience. I did not know it would last a lifetime.

A few elders of the earlier generation in the field of Punjabi letter—Gurbux Singh, Dhani Rama Chatrik, Principal Teja Singh—merely smiled. Two of them passed away. Gurbux Singh decided to create a world of his own—which had little to do with all that was happening around him.

Deep down in the layers of my mind, was the first impact of a religion against which I had risen as a child, when I had seen that glass tumbler touched by someone with a different faith became impure.

This broadened the outlook of my innermost eye, and even after having suffered so much from the Partition, I found it within me to deplore dispassionately the holocaust caused by the devotees of the two religions. Thus it was that I came upon that painfully sensitive face around which my novel *Pinjjar* (Skeleton) was written.

I had hardly stepped out of my teens then. I saw in that face the embodiment of the man of my dreams. (I wrote about him at some length in *Akhari Khat.*) It was like leaping into the flames every day. I was worn out by the effort and when someone telephoned to give me the news of the Akademi Award in 1957, my first thought was: 'Lord! I didn't write *Sunehre* for an award! If the one who had inspired me hadn't read the book, did it matter at all to me if this entire world had?'

Late that evening, came a reporter and a photographer from the press. The photographer wanted me to pose as one engrossed in the act of writing. I put a sheet of paper on the table in front of me and, pen in hand, began writing in a trance, the name of the one for whom I had written *Sunehre*. 'Sahir, Sahir, Sahir . . .' I had completely filled the sheet with that name.

When the pressmen had gone and I was alone, it struck me: 'What if in the photo that would appear in all the papers the next morning, the incantation "Sahir, Sahir, Sahir . . ." would show?'

It was like living through the classical romance of Majnu madly calling out 'Laila, Laila, Laila . . .'

But in the photograph my hand had obscured the sheet of paper on which I was writing. Not a squiggle of what I wrote was to be seen in the morning papers. Momentarily, I was relieved. But then a cry of anguish when . . . God knows it wasn't true . . . it wasn't!

I have carried a little more of Sahir into the novels *Ashoo, Ik Si Anita,* and again in *Dilli Diyan Gallian* through the character of Sagar.

I wrote also, poems. *Sunehre* till then, was the longest— longest in fact of all those under the title *Chetter.* After an exile as it were of fourteen years, I felt at long last that I was through with this phase of my life.

Yet the years one has lived through are not like the clothes one wears. Constrictive corsets leave marks that might mar the beauty of a sensitive complexion, but the scars left by the years that one lives through, are infinitely deep . . .

Much later, when I was at Varna, a city south of Bulgaria, flanked by the sea on one side and mountainous forests on the other, my wild imagination conjured up a ship sailing towards the shore and from the ship he seemed to have alighted and entered through the window of my hotel room . . .

The real and the illusive so intertwined, I sat up and wrote the poem beginning with the line:

Long have thoughts of you lain in exile.

The curse of my lonesome state has been broken through . . . by Imroz. But before I met him, I had the privilege of a friendship with a wondrous soul. Sajjad Haider had come into my life before the Partition. I had, however, never so far come across anyone who had not brought complications and misunderstandings in his train. Bitterness had been shed all around by litterateurs . . . barring, of course, Sajjad. He was perhaps the first real friend I had.

As long as I was in Lahore, we met often enough and talked—yet only as occasion demanded. He carried with him always an air of respectability. Soon after the riots began, dusk-to-dawn and then all day curfews followed. But at whatever time the curfew was lifted, he would come—no matter for how brief a while. In between came April 23 and my little daughter's first birthday. With arson and rioting all around, there was no thought whatsoever of a celebration. Yet whose was that knock at the door? Sajjad's. He had braved all and come with a birthday cake for her.

The riot-torn month of May 1947 took me for safety to Dehradun. Letters from Sajjad came regularly nonetheless. Then, at about the time my son was born, Sajjad also became a father at Lahore. I named my son Navraj; Sajjad found a name sounding nearly alike for his, Navi. We saw each other's sons through the photographs we exchanged.

One day Navraj had fever. My anxiety grew with the days. When I found the time to reply to Sajjad's letter, I happened to mention something about the little one's fever. The letter I received by return post is still engraved in my memory. He had written: 'I have been praying all night for your son. There is an Arabic saying: "when the enemy prays, the prayer is bound to be granted." In the eyes of the people I am an enemy of your country at this hour . . . God forbid that I ever become one of ours or your child's . . .'

My poem about the partition—*To Waris Shah*—came after I had written *Neighbouring Beauty*. This poem I had sent to Sajjad. As chance would have it, I lost the Punjabi version. That explains why it has never been published in my language. Sajjad, however, translated it into English and had it published in *The Pakistan Times*.

Seven years after I had met Sahir, I wrote a poem *Seven Years*. Even though he was in India, I had not had the occasion to meet him. When published, *Seven Years* somehow found its way to Pakistan. On reading it, Sajjad wrote to me. 'I want to come to India to see you. I want to talk to you of him for whom you've written *Seven Years.*'

Sajjad was in Delhi for a good eighteen days. Nights he spent at Marina Hotel, days at my house. This was the first time in my life I realized I had a friend in the world, a friend in every sense of the word. For the first time ever it dawned on me that a poem does not need to be created out of the passion of love. It can waft across the calm seas of friendship. At parting, I wrote:

Buy me a pair of wings, Stranger—
Or come and live with me

Once at a party in Lahore, the wife of a friend of Sajjad's again and again came around to him with a plate of *amrita* sweets. He laughed the offer away a couple of times, then soberly commented, 'Sister-in-law, I've allowed you to joke at her expense this time—but don't dare do it again. How little you know of the devotional quality of my love for her!'

Another incident comes to mind. We had just returned home in Patel Nagar from Connaught Place by rickshaw. The rickshaw-man demanded a little more than his due. I was about to protest when Sajjad paid off the amount claimed and after the man had left, observed in a philosophic vein: 'I feel I owe something to every refugee from Pakistan.'

If only the world of politics had shown such an attitude—or even an infinitesimal part of it! The lines of communication between the two countries were snapped. In my most difficult years, when I felt so isolated, I had not even the consolation of a word from Sajjad.

By the time Imroz came along, for a while the channels of communication between the countries were reopened. We wrote a joint letter to Sajjad. Salutations from world historians must, I felt, go with the reply that followed. 'I have not had the pleasure of knowing you, my friend, but I can from a composite picture from Ami's (the name he called me by) letters. Your rival salutes you.'

In due course, Imroz and I together met Sahir, who was rather ill-at-ease the first time. The empty glasses we had drunk from, remained long on his table. Late that evening he wrote the poem *Mere Saathi, Khali Jaam.* He read it out to me over the phone at around eleven that very night and also related how he was pouring liquor into each of the three glasses in turn and quaffing the contents. Imroz was down with fever in Bombay during the next meeting. Promptly, Sahir sent his own physician to attend on him!

Thoughts of Sajjad have unabashedly come out of my pen—although the political situation is such that I should not mention his name. In the course of recent TV and radio interviews, memories of Faiz returned, and of Nadeem, and of course, Sajjad. Some Pakistani intellectuals saw my repetition of these names as evidence that we had not accepted the reality of Partition; that in fact, we were not recognizing the cartographical fact of Pakistan, that our souls and spirits were restless and so on and so forth . . . The sum total of this was that Sajjad wrote to me saying I must never, even indirectly, refer to his name in my subsequent radio and TV sessions. From the depths of my depression I can only bring myself to say: 'My friend! Your name comes to my lips today since otherwise my recollections would remain incomplete. But God forbid, should you consequently happen to feel any embarrassment, I could never forgive myself. In the name of amity, not a whiff of the scorching winds of politics must so much as touch a pure soul like yours!'

As a result of newspaper reports about the controversy, they arranged a discussion through the External Services channel of Delhi Radio. Among those on the panel were the principal of Jamia Millia Islamia, a lecturer, and I. The topic was—what were our feelings about the separation of Pakistan from India? My only regret is that there is so little recognition of such a thing as friendship. The three of us did our best to clarify this one and only one point during the half hour at our disposal. Whether this had any effect on them is not for me to assess. All I can say for the three of us is that we felt considerably relieved after the exercise. Sajjad should have too. But did he? This I ask as a sincere well-wisher of his.

An Aura of Silence

Oh, the pain of it as I look back on those days before Partition! The very air was rent with the most fantastic rumours. Apart from my marriage, I had not been involved in any noteworthy incident. Engaged at the age of four, I had been married off at the age of sixteen in the usual manner. But in literary circles, romantic fireworks began to be sparked off. I learnt that Mohan Singh, the most revered poet of the time, had written some verses about me.

Speaking for myself, in whichever gathering I had the occasion to see or meet him, I had exchanged with him a few polite, perfunctory words at the most. No more. That was perhaps because of his rather aloof manner. I had nothing to fear from him of course. What I did fear was the sort of story that had started circulating. I gave him the reverence due an established poet. Nothing more. I was then being swamped by the lengthening shadows darkening my own mind. I was of course feeling not a little concerned about my being talked about in so glib a manner. Yet I had no reason to complain of him. Mohan Singhji was a thorough gentleman, with a suavity all his own. One evening, he came along with a friend (Dr Divan

Singh, I think, but I cannot be sure of the name), to see me. By the following morning, as rumour had it, he had written his poem *Property* that began—'She stood silently in the doorway . . . on the threshold like a piece of a master's possessions . . .'

I was passing through a phase of mental agony those days since rumours like this, without rhyme or reason, gave rise to all sort of conjectures. I was struggling to break through my silence although Mohan Singhji never lost his tongue in my presence. This silence however, as I reckon it, bespoke of both his dignity and grace.

One day, Mohan Singhji turned up with another friend— the Persian scholar, Kapur Singh. I was shy as ever, partly out of courtesy but partly perhaps because I was basically rather unforthcoming in my attitude. Kapur Singhji suddenly observed: 'Mohan Singhji, don't misunderstand her. She doesn't love you.' The deep and long silence melted. I took courage to declare, 'Mohan Singhji . . . You have all my respect. I am a friend of yours . . . What more do you want?' I thought I had said enough. Mohan Singhji had nothing to say to that. He wrote a small poem afterwards with the same refrain. 'You have all my respect . . . I am a friend of yours . . . What more do want?' The next line spoke out with a hollow voice: 'Aye, what more do I want?'

Rumours nonetheless kept circulating by word of mouth, and through sly digs in various pieces of writing. But nothing from Mohan Singhji's writings caused me any pain and my respect for him in no way diminished.

In passing, another incident comes to mind. A certain officer of the Lahore Radio Station was versed in literature. A confessional suddenly came from him directly after I had finished my programme: 'Had I met you years back, I would have sought release from my Muslim religion to Sikhism . . . or else you would have been a convert . . .' These words rose with the wind and died with it. It was the spell of a fleeting moment, without a beginning and without an end. Nothing more was ever said by him. Yet stories began to be spun out of the little he had said. Perhaps he himself gave cause for the stories. I heard and read quite a few twisted versions. So often have I felt since, that some Punjabi writers have no depth from which their writings can take shape. They create the stories and then work themselves up to relish the romantic fancies they embellish their stories with.

Years later, when I worked at the Delhi Radio Station, I came across Pandit Satyadev Sharma, who incidentally had served as staff-artist at the Lahore Radio Station before he took up work in Delhi. He wrote a story in Hindi titled *Twenty-six Men and a Girl.* He had been influenced in this by a story of Gorky's. His was really only another variation on an earlier theme. So when he read it out to me, he related in detail how many had been interested in me, with special reference to that officer, and how everyone eagerly watched, month after month, for developments they imagined would follow. The anticlimax was, there were no developments.

Sharmaji would perhaps never have written that story had his memories not been stirred up by sight of me. Innumerable petty characters, with ears to walls in the vain hope of having something fresh to regale each other with, filled the story right through. Hearing nothing, they kept falling back over each other imagining that they were alas too late to smack their lips on the juiciest bits.

Sharmaji was a very ordinary writer. But even the most ordinary writer can sometimes write a masterpiece. This was his. He had made an all-out effort to describe a thickening atmosphere. The marvel was that he had not, like those Punjabi writers, come to any forced conclusions. Through the simplicity of the treatment, the truthful character of the writer reached the reader.

The Cycle of Hatred

This too is a simple, straight incident basically; only it becomes deviously mixed up in an ever-widening web of hatred. There was a certain Punjabi poet. I had never come across him. It was during the earlier years of my literary career at Lahore. I had heard often enough of what he was in the habit of fabricating against me. Never having met him, I often wondered what the cause of his animosity was. Just before Partition, I contracted fever. The editor of a weekly came to inquire about my health. A man accompanied him whom I had never seen before. On his introduction, I sat bolt upright in consternation. He was the one who could not stand my very existence. What baffled me was why he had come to my sick bed.

Two or three days later, I read a poem of his in the weekly. Beneath was published the date of his visit to me. A strange passion. Just as there was no justification for his animus, there was none for his new pose of friendship. When he took the liberty of repeated visits, I asked the reason for this sudden somersault in his character and attitude. I could never really get down to fathoming him. True, there was nothing loud or objectionable about him; indeed I detected a strain of sternness in the way he conducted himself. He also had about him an abominable air of superiority . . . as if everyone he came across was no better than a worm! While I wrote my periodic reviews for the radio, he would inflict himself on me and insist on dictating to me who exactly to include and who to leave out and how much was to be said about whom. So unbearable were his literary pretensions that I became rather impatient with him. I had barely begun to give vent to my feelings, when Partition happened. That released me from his intrusions. Years later, I heard that the eventful historical happening was because of the fact that I did not want such a friendship to grow! The blood of millions was shed to satisfy his perverted logic. Let psycho-analysts put such a mind to clinical tests if they will; I have nothing to say. Of course, I have occasionally read what he has continued to write about and against me. Its roots are to be found at the point where this cycle began.

1947

The most gruesome accounts of marauding invaders in all mythologies and chronicles put together will not, I believe, compare with the blood-curdling horrors of this historic year. Tale after tale, each more hair-raising than the last, would take a whole lifetime to retell. Uprooted from Lahore, I had rehabilitated myself at Dehradun for a while, but later went to Delhi for work and a place to live in. On my return journey, I could not get a wink of sleep on the train. The pitch-black darkness of the night was like a sign of the times. So piercing were the sighs the winds carried and echoed, it seemed we were back in mourning over this Watershed of History. The trees loomed larger and larger like sentinels of sorrow. There were patches of stark aridity in between like the mounds of massive graves. The words of Waris Shah, 'How'll the dead and departed meet again?' surged back and forth through my mind. I thought, a great poet like him alone could bewail the loss a Heer once had to bear. But who could lament the plight of millions of Heers today? I could think of no one greater than Waris Shah to chant my invocation to. In the moving train, my trembling fingers moved on to describe the pangs I went through:

> *From the depths of your grave,*
> *Waris Shah,*
> *Add a new page to your saga of love*
> *Once when a daughter of Punjab wept*
> *Your pen unleashed a million cries,*
> *A million daughters weep today, their eyes turned*
> *To you, Waris Shah.*

The published poem found its way to Pakistan. Later still, Ahmed Nadeem Kazmi disclosed in his foreword to a book by Faiz Ahmed Faiz, that he had read the poem in jail. On his release, he recounts having seen copies of it with common men who would weep when they read it.

At a BBC interview in London (1972), I was introduced to Sahab Kizilbash, the Pakistani poetess, who exclaimed: *'Arre!* So this is Amrita . . . the writer of those lines! I ought to be embracing her . . .!' At Surinder Kochhar's an evening later, Sahab and other Pakistani poets, Saki Farruqui, Famida Riaz, Abdullah Hussain, the famous author of *Udas Naslain,* Nizakat Ali, and Salamat Ali had assembled. The cultural life of London that night was enriched by much reciting of poetry. When it was Nizakat Ali's turn, someone pointed out that he had never recited without some instrumental accompaniment. Yet, for one who had written on Waris Shah, he was chivalrous enough to consent and his superb voice enriched the airs afloat that memorable night.

In 1975, Mashkoor Sabri, a famous poet from Multan came to Delhi for an *Urs* recital. He told us of the Waris Shah annual celebration at which a folk-art exhibition is held, folk-dances are performed, and folk-songs are sung. The climax of this cultural evening is a Poets' Symposium. This multifaceted programme ends with a half-hour recital of Heer-Ranjha. The grand stage (100' by 80') on which the Heer-Ranjha sets form the darkened background, gradually lights up showing Waris Shah arising from his grave. The sets then continue to change with the shifting light, to synchronize with the lines of the poem. The reverberating sound effects of the finale acclaim a new dawn awakening a new spirit of love.

It was ironically the same poem that a quarter of a century earlier had evoked so much censure and disapprobation, with the Sikhs holding me guilty of not having addressed my invocation to Guru Nanak, and the communists, to Lenin or Stalin. Many a poet conspired to rant against the poem itself . . .

In the totality of myself as a writer, the woman in me has had only a secondary role to play. So often have I nudged myself into an awareness of the woman in me. The writer's role is obvious. But the existence of that other being I have increasingly discovered through my creative works.

When she came to life, three distinct incidents come to mind. Paradoxically again, there was no possibility of finding a place for her as she exists in the world of creativity. This fact I can realize and assess since the distance of years alone can make possible such a vision.

The first time was when I was twenty-five years of age. I had no child until then. Very often I dreamt of one: a fair face with finely chiselled features looking into my eyes. I began to recognize it after its repeated appearances. I used to dream of it speaking to me—so I began to recognize the voice as well. In one of these dreams I was watering plants. From one of the pots, instead of a flower, the face would suddenly spring up. Aghast, I would ask: 'Where were you?' 'Right here!' He would break out into laughter with the reply. And I would hurriedly lift the little one from the pot.

But when I would wake up, I would find myself all alone—a woman in name, who, if she could not become a mother, could find no meaning at all in existence . . .

The second time was when Sahir had turned up with a fever. He had racking pain all over and was finding it particularly difficult to breathe. I rubbed Vicks on his throat and chest—in fact I went on and on, as if I could spend the rest of my life doing it. The mere contact had magnetically rendered me into a mere woman, with no need at all for paper or pen.

The third time the woman in me came to the forefront was when Imroz sat once, working in his studio. On completion of the canvas, he dipped the brush into the red paint and with the tip of it, dabbed a mark on my forehead.

This secondary role as a woman, however, rakes up no quarrels with my main being as a writer. Rather, the woman in me has in a disciplined manner learnt to accept that secondary role. Only three times over the years did she wish to assert herself and the writer move aside to make way for her.

A Debt

I know nothing about the Mutiny of 1857. But the word 'mutiny' had stuck somewhere deep inside me like a story from Grandmother's lips.

This word was associated with something alive—and as intriguingly at the same time, with something dead and buried. So many voices kept recurring from it, voices that I could neither define nor divine. They were human all right, but one got lost in another, one found another, each clashed against the other like swords and inflicted wounds that bled with all those thrusts and parries.

So many colours were drained out of this word, like blood glistening in the sun. But in the end it was all so hollow, dead. My thoughts would sometimes rally round it like ants quickening their movements over a dead body.

Only one sign of the Mutiny had I seen with my own eyes. The family I married into had inherited a carpet. A *sardar* had looted the priceless article in a melee at some place in Delhi. What colours were originally woven into it I cannot say, but I knew it as a faded, worn-out ancient mass of silk almost falling apart. Grandfather, however, always preferred to sleep on this relic when the family lived in Lahore.

During the mass exchange of refugees in 1947, the move to Delhi became inevitable. But the head of the family— Grandfather, that is—refused to leave. He could not bear to tear himself away from memories and possessions handed down from generation to generation. He had the firm conviction that the chaos and confusion would get sorted out in time. Governments could not seize peoples' homes. He wanted to stay back. But when conditions worsened, the military packed him off in a truck to Delhi. All that he could carry as bedding was the tattered silk carpet. The anguish of leaving behind all his treasures and belongings and the discomforts of the journey were too much for him. He lived only a few days after reaching Delhi. He was lying on that carpet when he died and after his death, it was given away to a *fakir*. One thought came to all members of the family: 'This carpet was looted from Delhi during the Mutiny. Today, accounts have been squared up. What belongs to Delhi has been returned to it after a century.'

If loot too is a sort of debt that one day has to be paid back, the fearsome thought that time and again surfaced in my mind was that I too might have to return something. What it was, to whom, and when, I could not guess.

Like a comb in tousled hair, my thoughts too would often get tangled. My mother's mother and her mother's mother— every woman's mother had looted the sixteen graces in some mutiny against society. Those graces and arts should have passed on from generation to generation. I had to repay that debt to society. How and when I still do not know. All I know is, some day I will have to render accounts. How many more women will, I cannot say. I cannot presume to comment on how they feel. But speaking for myself, I sorely feel the weight of that debt.

I had that sort of feeling long before Partition. Out of that very pain I had written a poem once:

Fellow-traveller, we are parting company today
This distance between us will grow . . .

But this distance was not related to any event. It was something personal.

This distance grew with an avalanche in 1960; I feared the self within would fragment. The voice from the depth of my heart could no longer go unheeded. And I thought, 'I cannot retain anymore what is due to my husband. I have stolen shelter under his roof. Like what was looted once in the Mutiny, I must return what is due to my husband. I must return to him what is his . . . I must . . . I must.'

To him, both ways were equally painful. The distance between the way our minds ticked and our nerves reacted was immeasurable. We could not work out a living together. Yet, must we carry on because it was the socially acceptable thing? There had to be another course. Between the two, after due deliberation, I thought it better, and so chose in all honesty, the second.

Neither of us had any grievance against the other. The decision was reached after long discussions in a friendly fashion. The question of any humiliation for either of us at any stage did not arise. What we had gained from each other, was undeniable; what could not be had, was no ground for unpleasantness. What was imperative was the distance between us to be recognized. A genuine need for the acceptance of that fact had arisen. To my mind, it was in the interest of both.

We divided the areas of anguish. But our expressions were immensely relaxed because of the candour of our approach. There was really no need to conceal the pain of parting. And so we accepted it, as we did each other's features and form, warts and all, as a constituent factor in the reality of our existence.

We took it to be a strange enough way out anyhow. Nothing was said about laws and courts. Nor was it at all necessary. We were far too immature when we were married. But the supremacy of law could not be denied. When the parting came, the truth that had to be faced by both of us was stronger than any code of law.

I have been treated better by fate than the fellow-traveller I had parted with. In the years that followed, I had Imroz; he has had only loneliness. Fate has also been all too frugal in giving him anything that gives life a meaning.

We still meet but like friends, fully aware that loneliness cannot be got over with in such meetings. I bow my head low before anyone who has to bear the curse of solitude . . .

I have nonetheless a sense of pride in this bowed head of mine. I have not had to pay the price of security. I have not allowed the prestige of family life to suffer, nor have I fallen for any of the usually accepted social sanctions. I have always had, in the course of my journey over each milestone in life's mutiny, the realization of having been able to pay back the debts I owed.

What usually happens in such cases did not happen to me. Characters in a story have normally roles of protagonists or antagonists. Some remain in the periphery even though they share or are the cause of the sufferings of the central characters. In my case, those, who for years have risen up in arms against me are ironically the ones who have had nothing to do with the tenor of my life.

Some of my contemporaries had nothing to do with me and so could not have even recognized me had they passed me by in the street. To a certain extent, Punjabi journalists fall in this category. (A contemporary of mine went to the length of imploring my fellow-traveller to sign a paper so I should for the rest of my life be plagued by lawyers and court cases). But those woven in the warp and woof of my story followed the pattern of their lives in the silence of suffering that knows no words. Should we by chance meet after some time, our eyes fill with the sacred tears of love and respect. So much so that even today, my sight is dimmed by the tears of parting.

The one exception to these antagonists has been Davinder. While I had no idea as to whom *Kalam da Bhedh*—his book on me—was dedicated ('To the mind and threshold of a door that would always remain open for Amrita'), he had, with deep reverence, gone ahead to present the first autographed copy to the person from whom I had separated. He fully understood that separation had not meant that we were not to extend common courtesies to each other. On the contrary, at an hour of a child's need or over a problem concerning my income tax—even otherwise, after every few days—we would call each other on the telephone. If ever anyone outside the family has understood such plain dealings, it has been the Australian writer, Betty Colin, who in times of distress trots along for advice to her friend, her divorced husband—indeed, whose second wife rings Betty up whenever she is disturbed over the very same man. To share tea and sympathy!

Such plain dealings have to be lived through to be appreciated fully.

An Exhumation from a Grave of 1959

The first raw deal that had left him stupefied, Father used to relate repeatedly, was at the hands of a devotee in Gujranwala, his hometown. Before going abroad, he had left in her safe custody a chest full of the treasure he had inherited: jewellery and gold *mohurs*. And, without batting an eyelid, the woman had on his return blandly asked him, 'Which chest?'

I seemed to have gone though a similar experience in 1959: 'I saw a devotee in the same revered seat, with whom I had deposited my basket of trust, and who was now as tersely shrugging me off with, "What trust"?'

Such dealings had left me stunned. Deep darkness, like a cloud, blanked everything out; the oppressive atmosphere would not disperse. I had reposed much love and faith in that sweet face of hers. Like somebody gazing into the ever-changing pattern of clouds, I have since wondered whether the clouds in the sky were formed to awaken memories of trust betrayed.

It was as if I had been pricked sore all over. Each such experience of mine found an outlet in a story—*Kale Akhar, Karma Vali, Hath Toka, Kaile da Chilka,* and so on. The character, Shanti Bibi, in the novella *lk si Anita* somehow could not express all that was welling up in me. I therefore felt compelled to write a fairly longish story *(Number 5),* so that the lack I had in mind could be dealt with to some extent.

She was a child of tender years when I first met her. (A fuller sketch of hers is drawn in *Do Aurtan: Number 5*.) At the time of her marriage, I gave her whatever ornaments I had on me from the day of Partition. Not that I regretted parting with what little I had. What mocked at me in the raw weather was the glint and tinkle of those trinkets . . . as if bits and pieces of broken trust danced weirdly and scoffed at me in the surrounding darkness . . .

I had strung her child's prattle on a silken skin and hung it around my neck. Lord Shiva had garlanded himself with snakes, surely not under the illusion that they were skeins of silk. And I wondered why Lord Shiva had hung his fate around my neck . . .

I had the sensitivity to react to the faintest of odours . . . and I simply could not stand stinking lies . . .

Even Father could not. I had observed that fact in childhood. He was tutor to a young man from Sialkot who lived under our roof until a job was found for him. But the man one day tore off part of what was written on a sheet of paper and inserted a certain figure (I cannot recall exactly how much) in the blank space above the signature. That amount, he said, was due him. He did not stop at that. He went further and filed a lawsuit for non-payment of the debt. And I used to call that man 'Uncle'! A pain similar to the one I had seen in Father's expression then, I had in 1959.

I wondered how close a resemblance experience can have. I too had paid for this child's education and had her living with me just as Father had a relative's son in the house. Later, Father had bought some land at Hazari Bagh, and had plans of raising an orchard. He had taken the boy with him. But the project did not work out. Father contracted typhoid, from which he did not recover. I got a few letters about that landed property for a while. Then followed dead silence. The trustee had illegally disposed off the property and pocketed the money. Thinking of him, and of her, I find myself muttering again and again. 'How could anyone? How could . . .?'

That was the moment in 1959 when I saw the last of her. A star had fallen from the sky—the star of truth.

1960

This is the saddest year: like a torn page from the calendar of my life. Having taken a decision, my mind had leapt over the threshold, yet tremblingly I did not know which way to go.

I had just about stretched my hand to pick up the phone to put a trunk-call through to Sahir, when I was flabbergasted at finding myself glaring at a page in *Blitz*. It blared forth the news—supported by a picture of his and his newly found friend. My hand stood suspended in the air inches away from the dial; my mental state corresponded to that of Oscar Wilde's:

> I determined to commit suicide. After a time that evil mood passed away, and—made up my mind to live, but to wear gloom as a king wears purple: never to smile again: to turn whatever house I entered into a house of mourning: to make my friends walk slowly in sadness with me . . .

Some people advised me to forget all this. It was ruinous advice. It would mean—the beauty of the sun and the moon, the music of daybreak and the silence of great nights, the rain falling through the leaves, or the dew creeping over the grass and making it silver—would all be tainted for me . . . to deny one's experience is to put a lie into the lips of one's own life. It is no less than a denial of the soul.

It was still vacillating in my friendship for Imroz. My saddest verse belongs to this year. I vividly recall a weird dream I had. I was sitting in a moving train. Opposite me was an aged man with flashing, piercing eyes. I kept turning over the pages of my book as he began to talk:

'Have you ever seen a black rose?'

'A black rose? I don't think I have!'

'A path from the next wayside station leads to a small village. I know of a rose garden there with a few red roses, a few white . . . but the rest of the vast field is full of deep black ones . . .'

'Really!'

'Do I appear reliable enough to you, or do I not?'

'Have I said anything that makes you ask that question?'

'Would you like to see that rose garden with your own eyes?'

'I was wondering whether I could . . .'

'There is a myth about it . . .'

'And that is . . .?'

'Should you make up your mind, I'd rather relate the story there itself.'

'Sure.'

We got down at the next station. Picking our way along a fairly long half-beaten track, we discovered to our dismay that no transport was available. But eventually, we got to the place we had set out for. Such winsome beauties I had never before imagined could exist anywhere in the world. There was a bright red patch; there was also a milky-white one, but what melted the sight was acre upon acre of deep black blooms melting into the horizon.

'And now the story . . .'

'A fair lady, so at least goes the legend, was pure of heart and . . . as pure of soul . . . One day, he, whom she loved, decked her hair with a damask rose, and she wrote and sang sweet and soft airs.

'The course of true love did not run smooth, and the lady spent the rest of her life thinking about what makes things go wrong. And verse after verse she wrote from the depths of her broken heart.

'Only those who have felt deep pain can understand the suffering of others. Merging herself in that general suffering, she continued to write of depths unfathomed . . .'

'And then what happened?'

'She died . . . and was buried here. And then as if by magic, three roses—one red, one white, and one black, came forth from her grave!'

'Strange . . . Incredible!'

'The bushes kept getting bigger and bigger. Not a soul was around to bud or prune them . . . no one to water them. Yet they kept growing till the rose garden you see, took shape . . .'

'Oh And what have people to say to that?'

'They say the red blooms shot up from the love-poems; the black ones from those of pain; and the ones she wrote out of compassion for all, were milky-white . . .'

A shiver went right through me. I brought myself to ask: 'And will you not tell me your name?'

'My name? Er . . . well, call me if you must . . . Time.'

'Time! How's that? How can you be digging out of me the story of my own life?'

Time's smile and my own shiver then woke me up from my sleep . . .

And I wrote: 'When you cannot fill the goblet of night with the nectar of life: when you cannot taste the honey life offers you, you cannot call it tragedy . . .

'Tragedy is, when the silver plating peels off and the contents of the bowl turn poisonous and penetrate into your imagination . . .

'Tragedy isn't, when fate cannot read the address of the one you love, and so your life's letter goes undelivered . . .

'Tragedy is, when you write your life's letter to your love and you yourself go and lose his address . . .

'Tragedy isn't, when social and other ties strew the long road of your life with thorns and nettles, and your feet bleed sorely . . .

'Tragedy is, when with sorely bleeding feet you stand where no pathway opens before you . . .

'And tragedy isn't when you keep covering the shivering, cold form of your love with ragged verse . . .'

Towards the end of that year, I underwent treatment at the psychiatrist's . . . really to get to know myself. I read the standard books on psychology. At the instance of the psychiatrist, I put down on paper, to the extent I could, all my dreams . . . some of which I still remember:

I stand on the top of a tower, all by myself, talking to the pen I have in hand, 'Will you always be with me? Always?'

Suddenly someone clutches my hand.

'You're an illusion. Let go of my hand!' Sternly I command and breaking myself free, flee down the stairs . . .

No matter how fast I speed, the stairway goes on and on . . . Down and farther down I go, gasping for breath . . . yet I dare not stop, or I will be swooped on from behind.

Finally, I reach the landing . . . and there spreads before me a fantastic garden . . . with a whole sea of thronging crowd! Was it a fair-ground right round the base of the tower? There was a spectacle of some kind at one end: at another, a match.

Suddenly out of nowhere I spot an old bicycle of mine. Grabbing it, I hop onto the saddle . . . trying to find a way out. But whichever direction I take, again and again I come up against a stone wall. When I wake up I still have this maddening feeling of wanting to escape and not being able to . . .

A huge statue of white alabaster lies flat at my feet. Looking at it in dismay, I finally accost it with the words: 'What do I do with you? You have not the breath of life in you; you cannot speak! I'll break you to bits! I'll pack you off right away. You've wasted all my life . . . You . . . My image! My ideal! . . . Mastering all the strength I have in me. I hurl it away . . .

And with that my dream breaks.

A damsel of twenty years or so, stood by my side. She was the very picture of perfection. But she was ebony-black, carved out of black marble . . .

'Who is she now?' someone asked of me.

'My daughter.'

'Come now! You're pulling a fast one on me, aren't you? I've seen both your children. So fair . . . so charming they are . . . but this one . . .'

'The fair ones are small . . . She is the eldest . . . Do you know something about the manifestation of my art? The Goddess Parvati was churned from my wrath. And do you know that her son Ganesh was in turn kneaded from the dough of her own body?'

I passed through a desolate region with neither face nor form in sight. A voice came to my ears. It was a song, 'you've been the undoing of me, Sahiban, You've hung my arrows on a silver.'

'And who are you?' I looked around on all sides and asked.

'I am the valiant Mirza. Sahiban, my beloved, went and hid my arrows . . . That was not fair . . . the way she had me shot dead . . .'

I again looked all around. Seeing no one, I said: 'Stories have a way of changing sides . . . Today a certain Mirza has gone and hidden my arrows . . . is it fair . . . the way he has had a courageous woman like me shot dead . . .?'

The clouds thunder and roar. The sky shakes with wind and rain. A jagged streak of lightning flashes through the sky and falls on my right hand.

The shock of it goes right through my body. When I regain balance, I look at my hand and shake it. It is a relief to find only a slight scratch, from which oozes a drop of blood.

Another peal of thunder, and on the same hand, strikes lightning again. Recovering from it, I examine the hand. A slight scratch . . .

Thunder and lightning a third time. Now I cannot move my hand—one finger is bent. Holding the parallel finger of my other hand as a supporting splint, I press it hard again and again. It straightens out—as before. And as a last test, I take up my pen. I can still write, as well as ever. My mental state at the time is like Baudelaire's in his *Ode to Beauty*.

On the eve of Republic Day the same year I was deputed to go to Nepal. I was still a mental wreck when I wrote the following two letters to Imroz:

Yesterday Nepal honoured the same pen with which I had written my love-songs for you. All the flowers showered upon me are therefore my offerings to you. How did some light kindle this inky night of separation? Thoughts of you will ever remain lit in this poem of mine. Talk of this light— and much more besides, went on until as late as late could be. A Persian poet's lines come to mind:

Under the desert sun they run.
The shimmering sands as though water,
But the tortuous illusion soon passes.
'How can sand shine,' wise men opine—
'Blinding sand's continuity
Confine them?' But the thirst of those
Must, say I, first be seen—how it goes.

I might have illusions about my wisdom, but not of my thirst . . .

January 27, 1960

Wayfarer! Why did you the first time meet me at an
evening hour!
I am approaching the turning point of my life.
If you had to meet me at all why did you not meet me
at high noon
When you would have felt its heat.

The Hindi poet, Shiv Mangal Singh Suman, read this poem.
Each feels his own pain. But sometimes such pains bear striking
similarities. These longings of mine have been bruised against
that stern citadel of yours in the same city of my earlier hopes.
The first waiting too lasted a good fourteen years (like Lord
Rama's period of exile); the remaining years too might well
get added to those gone by . . .'

February 1, 1960

2

MEETING WITH CENTURIES

According to Hindu religion, each man must pass through four stages—four *varnas* and four *ashrams* in the course of his life span. I do not presume to know much about this. All I know is that in the course of my life's journey, I can discern four milestones.

During the first phase, like a *Bodhisattva,* I sat looking upon everything with an eye of a wonder: the minutes were somehow magnified, though for no reason that I can explain.

By the second, I had developed an overwhelming consciousness—it was the vigour of youth in revolt against the bastions of social tradition. The hatred and wrath rising up in me was like the precious stone in a toad's head.

The third one was the courage to forget and demolish the present and to build a new future, the courage to shuffle dreams like cards before they are dealt out . . . the courage to take the losses in a game and to shuffle the cards again and deal them out afresh in the hope that luck would change.

The fourth is this sense of isolation.

Three or four years back when Ho Chi Minh, the President of Vietnam, came to Delhi, he kissed my forehead and said: 'We are both fighting the wrong values, are we not . . .? You with your pen; I with my sword.'

Such was the effect of Ho Chi Minh's personality on mine, that I wrote a poem which was later published in the Vietnamese daily *Nham Dan* on May 9, 1958. I broadcast it along with my translations of popular folk-songs of the world from Delhi Radio Station. I dedicated *Aashma* to Ho Chi Minh himself— when later it was published in an anthology. Promptly, on March 1, 1961, he cabled back: 'I send my friendliest admiration and kindest greetings.' At that, part of my mental wrath subsided.

An episode from an English film comes to my mind. The ageing Queen Elizabeth I falls in love with a young man as she entrusts a ship to him. She sees him sailing away through a telescope and goes through hell's fire herself. His ladylove is by his side on the deck. Observing the impact of that scene on the Queen, a sympathizer advises: 'Will Your Majesty not look a bit higher?' Higher, above the heads of the two, flutters the flag of the Queen.

So I suggest to myself: 'Amrita, look a bit higher!' From that day, I have really and truly tried to look above the setbacks and anxieties of life, to my novels and to my poems . . .

It was my Russian friends who pulled me out of the quagmire of the mental condition I was fighting in those times. In March came an invitation from the Moscow Writers' Union and at the same time, a letter from the famous poetess, Zulfia Khanum, inviting me to be her guest in Tashkent.

On April 23, I arrived in Tashkent. Bits and pieces of some wonderful moments find expression in my diary:

Zulfia's heart bubbles like a goblet of wine with the exuberance of love . . . and on the table-spread stands a glass of the reddest pomegranate juice. Sipping from both I turn the pages of the books before me. The language poses the only barrier between us. On the jacket of a book is the profile of a young girl—a tear just about to drop from her eye. I feel the tear crossing that barrier and dropping on my lap. I observe 'I do not know why it must ever be so, Zulfia, tears in the eyes of any woman establish a relationship with women the whole wide world over.'

When the tears are understood, the relationship deepens, does it not? Zulfia carried on in the imaginative strain. 'For me, Amrita and Zulfia are but two names of the same woman.' She reads out some verses by the nineteenth century poetesses, Nadira and Mahjuna . . . and for a good while we sit under the spell of silence they cast over us both.

At Samarkand, a poet, Arif, brought me two *lalla* flowers this morning. Both the flowers were exactly the same shade of red and sweet of scent. Zulfia and I exchanged the flowers offered just as we in our parts customarily exchange veils to establish bonds of friendship. Zulfia remarked, 'Two flowers, but the same scent; two countries, two languages—but the one link that binds us two is friendship, is it not?' A moment later, she thought up something more. 'But we don't find any stain of the pains in our hearts in these flowers, do we?'

I recalled the line in Nadira's poem in which she beseeches a nightingale to draw on her lamentations when it has finished the songs swelling up in its throat. To which I added, 'And I'll tell the flowers to take upon their petals the stains of pains from Zulfia's heart and mine.'

'There are some *lalla* flowers that have black centres,' Zulfia said. 'Do let's go to the fields and pluck those.'

We both spent the rest of the morning in search of flowers with centres symbolic of our own condition.

Nabi Jan, our Uzbek interpreter, was accompanying us. He sought out the rarest of the *lalla* species, and holding one out to me, said; 'This one bears not the stain of pain you seek, but the peculiar sheen that comes on with light. Isn't that better?'

From deep down there shot forth glints of light when he smoothened some petals on the palm of his hand. Thanking him for putting us wise on that, I turned to Zulfia: 'That's perhaps because some memories of pains have their own flashbacks.'

She smiled. 'But aren't these memories of our own miracles? Were it all left to men . . .'

Leaving the menfolk out, we talked at length of our own miraculous powers.

When we returned to Tashkent, Ali Sardar Jafri, the Hindustani poet, had also arrived. Zulfia invited him to dinner at her house. Holding up her glass, she said: 'We call a girl "Khan", but "Khanum" when she grows up. So Amrita is for us Amrita Khanum. Translating "Amrita" into Uzbek, the word would be "Ulmus". I, therefore, raise this toast in honour of Ulmus Khanum!'

In return, Jafri translated Zulf into 'Alkh'. Hindizing it, he returned the toast in honour of 'Alka Kumari'.

When it came to my turn, I read the lines of a verse which came to me spontaneously:

When pen embraces paper, earlier silences are forgotten
Love reveals its secrets;
In Uzbek or in Punjabi, the rhyme is the same.

The name of a valley in Uzbekistan, Khabida Husina *(Sleeping Beauty* in translation) in conformity with the pattern of the current scene, has been changed to Fargana. Silk mills have been set up there. The local people now say that with so much silk being spun, just one year's output of thread would be enough to reach the moon. The directors of the mills, all women incidentally, took us around. At the end of the visit, they presented me with a fine piece of silk and asked if I had any message for the following day which was May 1—the day that has a special meaning for workers throughout the world:

Spinning your silk—oh Lass of this Vale!
May this May-day make all your wishes true;
Weaving your dreams—oh Lass of this Dale!
May your basket ever be full of my wishes for you!

Anna Khan pointed to the brandy, honey and pomegranate juice on the table and asked: 'What song—say honoured guest of ours, shall I sing for you?'

'Sing that song from your valley, Anna, that's as sharp in effect as that brandy, as sweet as that honey, and as full of love as that red juice over there . . .'

She and Lalla Khanum regaled me with song after song. The last one was a sole effort by Lalla: 'It's an honour to us— we've sought you out as our guest.' Moved to the innermost depths of my heart by this reception, I recalled a plaintive line of mine to the effect that Life had invited me to its house, but had forgotten to entertain me. I withdrew my complaint right there.

Zulfia was not able to accompany me and I travelled alone from Tashkent to Stalingrad. Many writers of Tadzhikistan— among them the very famous Mirza Tursungzade—were at the airport to accord to me a rousing reception. The introductions over, I said: 'My own salutations I offer to you all.' For Mirza's ears I add: 'But I also act as Zulfia's messenger in the words of our Urdu poet Faiz Ahmed Faiz: "The poet inscribed his *salaams* for you in the name of your beauty."' Mirza roars with laughter. 'Salaam Number One, from Zulfia; Number Two, in the words of Faiz; Number Three, presented by the Messenger I see . . .! Good gracious me! What'll happen to me!'

Twenty miles away from the town, on the hill-side on the bank of the river *Verz Aab,* are the writers' homes. *Verz Aab* means Dancing Waters. A dinner has been arranged on the river bank. In the name of peace and friendship, delectable toasts are drunk, and select verses recited.

It suddenly begins to drizzle. Mirza Tursungzade becomes thoughtful. 'The seed we've sown of our two countries' friendship needs to be watered. The sky descends to perform that deed!'

One poet seeks information. 'We've heard of a river in your country famed for its lovers . . . What may its name be?'

'Chenab . . . And you have Verz Aab. See how your river's name rhymes with ours!'

In Baku, the capital of Azerbaijan, 1 met some very fine people; especially the poetess Nigar Khanum, the authoress of around twenty volumes; Mirwarad Khanum Dilbazi; and the Persian poetess, Medina Gulgun. In the course of our poetry-reading session, I was reminded of Zulfia far away and read a poem of hers as well. The famous poet, Rasul Raza, raised a toast that is recorded still in my diary: 'Here now, five poetesses meet like the five rivers of Punjab—and I quaff deeply at the confluence!'

At this meet, a verse from the twelfth century poetess, Mehsati Ganjvi, was also recited. Calling it an Eight-Centuries' Meet, I took occasion to recall from an earlier verse of my own:

Because a drop of your love got mixed in my cup
I could drink the bitters of life . . .

and to observe:

But now a great many more drops are mixed . . .
And life's cup is a lot sweeter.

Travelogue

From the Ganges to the vodka,
Is this a travelogue of my thirst.

This journey brings back memories of my visit to other lands but the moment these recollections begin, there falls the shadow of my sadder days when it turns dark and the night is about to descend.

I was working for Delhi Radio Station then. Sajjad Zaheer came to my room, stood in a state of conflict as it were, and then said, hesitatingly, 'A delegation of Indian writers is to go to the Soviet Union . . . I want you to be one of us. No one from any of the other States raised any objection at the meeting yesterday, but there was a general chorus of dissent when it came to Punjab . . .' He added haltingly, 'They say that if Amrita is included in the delegation, their wives will insist on their withdrawal . . . I find myself in a strange fix . . .'

I have woven this tidbit, incidentally, in my novel *Dilli diyan Gallian,* page 77 . . . through the character, Raj Narain. When Sajjad Zaheer that day suggested that if I write a letter to the effect that I wanted my name to be included in the list of delegates, he would put it up to the higher authorities and see things through, I retorted: 'You've taken all the trouble to come, but how did you assume I'd be wanting to go? I have made up my mind. If at all I am to venture out to any part of the world one day, I shall go alone. Should the Russians want me to visit their country, they will send me an invitation. If they don't, so what?'

In 1960, the Moscow Writers' Union had asked me over; and in the following year I went to Tadzhikistan, Moscow, Tashkent and Azerbaijan.

In 1966, I travelled to Bulgaria on an invitation . . . and, of course, re-visited Moscow. Towards the end of that year, they were celebrating the 800th birth centenary of the Georgian poet, Shota Rustaveli. So I went yet again to Moscow, Georgia and Armenia. Alone.

In the course of the 1967 Cultural Exchange Programme, the Government of India sent me to tour Yugoslavia, Hungary and Rumania. After I had completed my three weeks' stay in each of these countries, the Bulgarian and West German governments honoured me by arranging similar tours in their countries. I was a guest for a few days at Teheran on my way back.

In 1969, I was invited to Nepal by our Embassy. And in 1972, in response to a special request, our government sent me to Yugoslavia under the Cultural Exchange Programme. Czechoslovakia and France were later added to my itinerary. On completion of the circuit, I went at my own expense to London and Rome. On an invitation from Cairo, I was able to spend a week there. On the occasion of the World Peace Congress, I visited Moscow again in 1973.

I do not habitually maintain a diary, but I do when travelling. The following are some passages from my travel diary.

May 24

How completely different are one's feelings when one is alone!
Looking out of the window by my seat as I fly, it seems to me
that the sky has been split into two pieces: one for me to lie on
and the other to use as a coverlet. The flight to Moscow will be
another two hours only, but I know not how long it will take
for me to reach my journey's end from this state of loneliness.

As far as the eye can travel, the earth appears to be sown
with patches of cloud scattered here, denser there. Just as Adam
was expelled from Paradise on his tasting the fruit of the earth,
so on tasting the moisture of the clouds, Adam has this day been
rocketted up from the earth . . .

May 25

I am stranded at the airport in Sofia. Someone suddenly plants
a bouquet in my hands and asks: 'You're Amrita, aren't you?'

I have just paid my homage to the national leader, Giorgi
Dimitrov, whose soul has merged into the spirit of the country
and whose body has been preserved with the help of science.
When Hitler had him arrested in 1933, the writers of the
country pooled all their resources to save him. The crusade
was led by that doyen of the French men of letters, Romain
Rolland. Together they fought free of the fascist stranglehold.
People hold Dimitrov in as high esteem as Indians do Nehru
and Gandhi.

May 26

I see the statue raised in memory of the soldier-freedom-fighters. Surrounding the monuments is the three-kilometre freedom-fighters' garden. The tortures and torments of a subject race and the longing for freedom are commemorated here.

May 27

I have had an interesting meeting with members of the Ministry of Cultural Relations and Foreign Affairs. Since they are all so understanding, I have felt free to talk about censorship and freedom of the press. 'So long as writers do not realize their responsibility, it is true that a lot gets written that ought not to be. But on the other hand,' I candidly inquire, 'what happens to those who have independent minds, who hold individual views?'

The reply is a considered one. 'Our Union makes allowances for that type of individuality. Expression of newer experiences is encouraged to a degree but for the establishment of a new tradition for the common good, untrammelled freedom can prove dangerous. On the whole, rather than have a sick literature, this policy is less harmful.'

Time cannot stop, I know . . . nor the questions coming up. But they will find a way out, even in a socialistic pattern of life. The questions and answers are exchanged in a pleasant atmosphere. Mr Stanchev concludes, 'We have reached from a rather low point to better heights. That shows some promise of reaching the best, doesn't it?'

I read some poems at a poet's meet. In turn, the French, Bulgarian and Russian language barriers break down in the endeavour to explore depths in the meanings of words. Yugoslav guest-poet, Zlatko Gorian, comes chivalrously to my rescue. He is a tried hand at translating from French to German. He places me under a debt of love with his parting words, 'Don't you now go and forget the Yugoslav who held out his helpful hand all through!'

I go round to see the historic homes of Iran Vazov and Nikola Vaptsarov, the famous Bulgarian writers. I have translated some of the former writer's poems years earlier into Punjabi. I find a book of mine at his place. Some of his lines that had stood still in my ears when I was going through the translating process, come out alive:

My faith
that tomorrow
life will be finer,
life will be wiser

My faith has strong armour
in my sturdy breast
and bullets that could shatter
My faith
do not exist,
do not exist!

He had written these lines before being killed by fascists in 1942. Reverently, I touch table, pen, teapot and other belongings with tears in my eyes . . .

A hundred and sixty kilometres away from Sofia, I stand in the village church where, in 1876, 2000 men, women and children took shelter against the invading Turkish hordes; and I look down into the well they dug with their nails to quench their thirst. They had all been barbarously killed by the invaders. As in Jallianwala Bagh in the Punjab, the walls too are perforated with bullets.

I see the printing press at Plovdin which the freedom-fighters used for publishing their underground literature; I also see the chains that held their feet, but not those of time—for time moved on.

Passing through Kalofer, I see for kilometres together, one long queue of people with bouquets in their hands, on their way to pay homage . . .

June 2 happens to be the anniversary of Haristobotev (birth or death?). This dearly loved people's poet had kissed his 20 days' old daughter and taken gun in hand to go out in defence of his country. He was barely 27 years old when he and his comrades-in-arms were killed—with the song he had written still on their lips. I have translated one of Haristobotev's poems this evening.

June 13

It has been raining hard all day. Not being able to go out, therefore, I sat in the room of my hotel and read a Bulgarian novel, *Under the Yoke*. I was startled at the heroine's name. It was Radha. There was even the more Indianized form *Radhika* at places! Over dinner, I humorously ask my interpreter: 'How's Radha a Bulgarian? Krishna was an Indian . . . or was it that she fled all the way from Bulgaria to meet him in India?'

June 14

At a farewell dinner by the Ministry of Culture and Foreign Relations, a few poets and poetesses—among them the famous Elissaveta Bagriana and Dora Gabe—were invited. Toasts were drunk. Dora Gabe raised one in honour of our Prime Minister, Indira Gandhi. Presenting some peacock-feather fans in the name of peace I said, 'These colourful feathers are of our national bird. We desire peace throughout the world so that our peacocks can go dancing all over.'

September 27

Moscow University is all aglimmer like a fairyland at evenfall. Standing at a vantage point opposite, I see the river encircling the entire city. The reflection of glowing lights in the flow of the water is a sight not to be forgotten: all the more beautiful because it has risen above the blood that has flown under, cutting through desert sands to satiate the hunger of the lands around . . .

The celebrations of the 800th birth anniversary of the dearly loved Georgian poet, Shota Rustaveli, began on September 25. How could those who had exiled him imagine that after a dip in time's ocean, his story would emerge with fairylike magic? During his lifetime, the very mention of his name was forbidden! That was why the people—two of whom, committed to memory the epic he had written—are honoured today.

The statue of a woman with sword in one hand and wine-cup in the other, is carved on the highest hill around Tbilisi. The sword is to protect the country from enemies, and the wine-cup held up to the country's friends! I also see the sixth century church, that in the eighteenth century was converted into a prison. Maxim Gorky had passed a term of imprisonment here.

A hundred and sixty kilometres out from Tbilisi, towards Barjomi Valley, we pass through Gori, Stalin's birthplace and visit the house in which he was born.

Writers from various parts of the world have arrived. At the meeting in the evening, everyone has something to say on the writer's role in improving the human condition. All hearts are touched when the Vietnamese poet, Chelin Vinh, gets up to speak: 'Our poetry is afloat in rivers of blood . . . today it speaks only of weapons of war so that a day will come when it can shower flowers on the waters. The poems we write are thrust into the pockets of our soldiers when they go out to fight

. . . in the fervent hope that those pockets are safe . . . for if we can save the poems, we'll think we've succeeded in saving mankind.'

He comes and sits by my side. 'Are you from India? Is your name Amrita?' he asks of me. Seeing me surprised, he says: 'When I was about to take off from Vietnam, Xuan Dieu, our outstanding poet, said to me: "If a woman comes from India, she's bound to be Amrita. Remember me to her."'

A prayer goes from my heart: 'If only all the poems of the world were to coalesce into one great poem, would that poem not stand in defence of Vietnam?'

October 2

I go around the museum of old manuscripts in Yervavan, the capital of Armenia. Nomads by tradition, some Armenians had written in Tamil when they had, in the course of their wanderings, settled down in southern India.

I have seen the thirteenth century church carved out of a mountainside. A stone stairway leads off into a maze. I am thrilled. Falteringly, I ask: 'Can I go up?' The maze seems to have a magnetic force about it. Yet, a little abashed, I answer myself: 'No! Perhaps I can't!' Seeing people kiss the altarstone, I think that I would not be permitted to place my foot on the sacred spot. But I am told, 'There is an alcove right up there, where chroniclers lit a lamp and wrote the history of Time as it passed. You are free to cross over, to sit and write for as long as you like!'

A British poet had asked me in Tbilisi: 'Have you ever been aware of a strange kinship with any of the peoples of the world?'

'Not quite that . . .' I had replied, 'but I have felt close to the characters of some books!'

The maze of the church in Yervavan has cast a spell over me. I think that not only characters from books, but some nooks and corners in foreign lands can be as familiar as those in my own country.

October 8, 1966

The 200 km road from Moscow is like a lovely arcade. I had heard of the marvellous Russian autumns. In full view before me are the broad russet leaves swaying with the wind from the branches of trees. With their stark white trunks, the trees look silver against their golden leaves.

I stand in Yasnaya Polyana, Tolstoy's house, where he wrote *War and Peace*. A white shirt hangs from a wall in his bedroom. As I lean on my arm, a breath of wind blows in from the window and the shirt sleeve touches me softly. It feels like the year 1910. . . For a moment, the hands of time turn anti-clockwise. I have swung from 1966. I am in 1910 . . . And lo and behold. Who do I see? Tolstoy himself in that very shirt!

Composing myself, I look around. Not another soul is there in the room. Only on the wall to my left hangs a white shirt!

August 26, 1967

Unfurling the banner with the inscription *Poetry is a Country without Frontiers!* they observe the annual festival of poetry at Struga on the banks of the river Drini in Yugoslavia. The first day is for poems in Macedonian; the second evening for those in the other languages of Yugoslavia, as well as for foreign ones. Poets stand in turn on the river's bridge to recite. The audience sits on the banks of the river and the boats float. The reflection of the flaming torches in the rippling waters is like some dancing dream from a fairyland. The poets recite in their various languages, and well-known actors of the country read out the translations, with a banner aloft of the country from which they come. I shall always remember this enchanting experience. There is deafening applause now as the names of Kalidas, Tagore and Nehru are mentioned.

August 30, 1966

In the car from Ohrid to Skopje the Ethiopian poet, Abre Zamberi, and Prince Mahteme Selaisse, are with me. Most of the way we spend talking of the Struga festival; during a halt over a mug of beer the Prince breaks down. 'You poets are the most fortunate folks . . . when the world around you is not to your liking, you have the capacity to create worlds of your own imagination. I spent twenty whole years playing the violin. I am in love with chords that can be turned into harmony. But since my right arm was shot up in the war, I have never played again. Music has lain frozen in my breast.'

History is silent. I am, too. A musician's hands were shot up . . . I brood over the reason, but find no answer.

August 31, 1967

Standing outside Kagujevac, about 100 kms from Belgrade, I see a vast expanse of green. In the blankness between, I see two white wings, about 18 yards in length, and ten yards above the ground. On October 21, 1941, the German force encircled a school here and shot down each child and teacher. The stone wings are a symbol of the plight of the 300 who lost their lives. The entire village population of 7000 fell victim to the same forces. The stone statues of a man and a woman stand as a symbolic monument over the 7000 graves. It strikes me standing here that the heartbeats of the dead have been embodied in the statues, or was it perhaps that a stone had entered those heartbeats, petrifying them?

September 9-22, 1967

I meet Vihar Bela, the Hungarian poet, who remarks, 'The moment an invader sets his foot on the soil of a country, the books are the first to start shrinking . . . But when a poet sets his foot on the same soil, the same books are again the first to swell out . . .'

After these first endearing words of welcome, I see the machine on which is inscribed Sandor Petofis' revolutionary poem, dated March 15, 1848. The poem is now the Hungarian National Anthem.

Deeply inscribed in my memory also is my meeting with Yobaj Karoj. Until Stalin's death, not a single book of his poems could be published. He had spent a four-year term in a Siberian prison. On his release in 1948, they discovered his poems in his pockets and packed him off once again—to a grimmer experience.

In selecting my poems for broadcast over Budapest Radio and for recitation at a writer's meeting, I am glad they have not asked me particularly for those with a socialist bias. They have accepted the ones I have chosen—for Sandor Rakos to translate also.

Meeting their famed poet Gabor Garai at the Union Office, I have occasion to meet again a French poet I had seen in Georgia a year earlier. 'Oh! that we could meet again in Paris next year,' he had written in my autograph book. When he reads my poems for the first time today, he beams, 'Thank God—these poems are *poems!* I was afraid you wrote poems only about socialism!' Upon this we all burst into laughter.

'We've been cowering for ten years in a cave of silence. It's possible now to write and publish what we feel,' said a poetess among us.

A hundred and twenty kilometres to the south of Budapest, I see the side of Lake Balaton where, on November 6, 1926,

Tagore had planted a sapling and had written: 'May this add to each new season of yours even when I have passed away from this earth.' A statue of Tagore stands nearby. The full verse inscribed on the pedestal is however dated November 8, 1926. I take a leaf off the tree and seem to read instead the date September 8, 1967 engraved on it . . .

The most coveted prize in Hungarian literature is the Attila Jozsef Prize named after their most revered national poet. Taking time off from the task of translating his poems, I go to the railway line where thirty years ago he had committed suicide. He was born, alas! at a time when individual freedom of expression was not tolerated.

October 9, 1967

I visit the church in Rumania where lies enshrined the skull of Calypso, the poor Greek girl who loved the Russian poet, Pushkin. A part of Rumania was at one time under the Turks. In 1832, when the people rose in revolt against the invading Turks, this girl was one of them. It was when these revolutionaries escaped to the southern parts of Russia, that she met Pushkin. But *Calypso* was the one poem for which the poet had no paper. So she returned broken-hearted. Since women were not permitted to enter that particular church, she went attired in the habit of a monk; and lived here till she committed suicide in 1840. Only afterwards, it is reported, did they discover who exactly she was, from the letter she had written and kept under her pillow.

I descend into the vaults. A sound travels to my ears, I cannot say whether it is the rustling in the trees made by the autumnal winds or Calypso's letter being unwrapped from the veils of time . . .

October 15, 1967

The habit I have formed of being able to work hard has paid off well today. I undertake to translate ten poems and stories of whichever country I visit. That is how I have come to understand many foreign writers. When I travelled from Rumania to Bulgaria the previous day, I learnt of our Prime Minister's presence in the capital. She has invited the President of the country to tea. As she introduces me to him, I am able to talk knowledgeably of Bulgarian literature. Both leaders are astonished at this.

October 26

On October 21, I am invited again by the local people of Kagujevac to read to them the Punjabi version of Desanka Maksimovic's famous poem on the occasion of the anniversary alluded to earlier. But following a rather tight schedule for nearly two and a half months, I have to defer this invitation to a later date. Germany now beckons me. As chance has it, I arrive there on October 21—a day associated with an atrocious crime by the German people. I feel terribly ill-at-ease with myself. But the Gior Boschner Award is being given to Heinrich Boel at Frankfurt, and I have been invited. I go straight from the airport to attend the function. I regain composure on hearing him say: 'You bestow this honour upon me for the manner in which I have given full rein to my feelings. But I do not feel happy . . . bombs are being rained on Vietnam and I am not able to do anything . . .'

I see the houses in which Goethe and Schiller lived. And I hear a philosopher comment: 'No poem or story can be written now in the language of a country that wrought so much havoc . . .' I muse, 'And this is a country associated always with thinkers and philosophers . . . Yet when there is still the capacity to feel with such depth, and still such awareness of guilt and crime, the same language can serve all sorts of expression.'

August 25-30, 1972

Returning a second time for the poetry festival at Struga is a memorable experience. The poets are interviewed. I am asked what the word 'freedom' means to me. My answer is clear— the system of government that gives meaning to the life of the commonest man, but without snatching away anyone's individuality.

I also see a stage erected in a historic church to salute the poet Pablo Neruda.

September 5, 1972

I take a glimpse of Pushkin's portrait at Montenegro. The poet had joined a gypsy-band and wandered off to this place at the age of sixteen. He felt so deeply in love with the place that he did not leave for a good five years. Pointing to his portrait, the Director of the Museum says to me, 'Pushkin stayed here for five years. How long will you, Amrita?' I laugh. 'The gypsy instinct in me will last, alas, for only twenty days!'

September 9, 1972

The people of Prishtina have an evening of my poems. The name of my country is splashed in bold letters, both inside and outside the theatre. Landscapes of India adorn the walls, and with the fanfare of Indian music, a proper atmosphere is created. My Yugoslav friend, Iliana Cura, wears a damask silk *sari* as she steps onto the stage to introduce me. I first read each of my poems in Punjabi, and the theatre actors then translate them into Serbian and Albanian. By chance, a visiting American poet, Herbert Kunner, happens to be present, but they cannot extend a direct invitation to him to recite. By tradition, the poet of the evening only can. So from the stage I request him to recite whatever he chooses to. The evening is rounded off with two short films: one on 'Khajuraho' and the other titled 'India on the Move'. My heart is full. So much have these people so feelingly and thoughtfully done for me.

November 10-16, 1972

In a way, each country is a poem in itself—some of the poem's lines are set in glittering gold; others steeped in blood shed by foreign guns; and some remain evergreen . . . yet there can be a country like an incomplete poem . . . Italy gives me the feeling of being both a complete and an incomplete poem. There are marble statues everywhere and I get the impression that they grow from the soil itself. The poems that fell into mines must have been quarried out as statues of alabaster; those which fell like seeds into the soil were tended by the hands of Michelangelo and other artists. The chapter of blood is a lengthy one when thousands of slaves like Spartacus played with each other's lives for the pleasure of the rulers and consuls of the day.

And there are poems pale as well—stricken pale from fear in front of the high walls of the Vatican ruled over by the Pope, poems crashing back to forever crouch within their own forms. Italy is a mighty land of destiny. Like the lushness around, there are poems which keep sprouting from the sap within, and like Dante, the writer of the Divine Comedy, who was exiled, there are those that got exiled as well.

But there are many other poems that will not be known by the tourist as he passes. They only smile as Leonardo da Vinci's enigmatic Mona Lisa continues to.

Kahira (Cairo) offers an experience unique in itself. I stand on the line that divides the land into two: one as green as green could be, the other a vast stretch of sandy desert, where stand the Pyramids that have been the diurnal course of 5000 suns. I remember an Arabic saying, 'The world might fear time; but time fears the Pyramids.'

A 500-Year Long Journey

Another moment—all smiles, from the beginning of the year
1969. It was a little after midnight when the telephone bell rang.
My son had put a trunk call through from Baroda University. In
reply to all the letters I had written, he came on the line, 'I'm
fine Mamma—in perfect health.'

That long-awaited voice pervaded my whole being.
Summer or winter, I use very light clothes in bed. I was asleep
when the telephone rang. Without thought of a wrap, I had
thrown aside my quilt and run to the phone. Yet I felt warm
enough. My flesh melted into my very spirit and fed the pure
naked soul to a flame.

As lightning in the dark, a thought flashed across my
mind—if I, an ordinary woman, could get a mighty thrill from
the sound of my son's voice, what must Mata Tripta have felt
during the time she was carrying Nanak?

The quincentenary of the Guru's birth was being celebrated
that year. I had just declined a request by my publishers for
a longish poem befitting the occasion. Had I got down to the
exercise earlier I might not have been able to transmute such
an experience as I had just gone through.

The moment had walked me five dark centuries back to
that worthy woman who had conceived Guru Nanak. In the
density of that darkness there was yet a soft glow for days and
nights on end. During this period, I literally lived through that
Greek saying 'All wood can be made into a cross,' and wrote

the poem *The Annunciation* in which the nine foetal months of Guru Nanak phase out into Mata Tripta's nine dreams.

Then followed that vilification through the columns of so many Punjabi journals, all urging the state government to ban the poem. I read and heard all that. One writer, Kirpal Singh Kasail, branded me 'love's worm' in the paper *Ajit* and questioned my right to handle so lofty a theme.

Other respected voices in Punjabi literature chose to remain tight-lipped on the issue. They allowed their responsibility to rest in silence.

Yet I did not feel lost. The creative moments I had lived through had given me the strength and joy to withstand all criticism.

At the same time I was aware of the powerful enemies I had made though I knew I would remain unhurt. While they were attacking me, I bore the cross I had made for myself until, through my suffering, I came to recover my usual calmness.

The Death of a Friendship

There was to be an end to the friendship, so it ended . . .
Good my friend!
Speak of it in amity or disdain
Whatever you feel . . .
It makes not the slightest difference now
If you enshroud it in splendid brocade or wretched rags.
Will I have to hear the entire story?
No—it's not Doomsday,
So it cannot be resurrected . . .

These lines were written some time at the end of March, 1971. A tenderly nursed friendship, a friendship that had been formed in 1966 and had conceived *Nagmani*. It died suddenly like in the failure of a heart. Four months after its collapse in 1970, the dirge quoted served only to strew one last handful of dust over its grave.

But it really is Doomsday today; Along with other graves, this too has yielded up its dead. I hear voices like the dirge of a Greek lament that goes 'Hallo, farewell!' The two moments— one of birth, the other of death—that had been buried in the grave, have been resurrected.

Strange, very strange. With what joy had the first moment come alive! And what sadness followed the second! Yet today, sadness had spent itself in the dirge. How paradoxical the resurgence of rejoicing over its death . . .

'I was simply an illusion, that is why I am sad . . .' a voice comes to my ears. Soon comes another, 'I have dispelled the illusion. That's why am I emancipated! That's why am I full of joy!'

It was the friendship of a budding Punjabi poet. One continues to wonder. When there is a shower the earth has an invigorating odour; contrarily, the earth could well be as stultifying as the dust after a period of drought.

I cannot run into stone until mankind does . . . I have not turned into stone since I can still see things with an eye of wonder.

I had got him a scholarship to study abroad. The face I had seen was not the same four years later when he returned. Many familiar faces seem strange with the passage of time.

My last words had been 'Friend! This is the most difficult day of my life. It's as if my own son or Imroz had returned from abroad, and for the sake of money had resorted to lies which strike me dumb. . .'

Only one word, 'Ami', the name by which Sajjad alone addressed me, cut tunnels through the rockiest of mountains to reach my ears. I was deprived of his comforting voice during the time of Partition when all lines of communication between India and Pakistan had snapped. I pleaded with Imroz in vain to call me by the same name. But no! He could not bring it to his lips. When in 1967 I went to the Eastern European countries, I met this friend in Hungary, in Rumania, and also in Bulgaria. He said something about Sajjad and me in the course of our conversation one evening, and on my yielding to his behests, began calling me by that name. The same quirk of fate that had in time made him a stranger, had got him to forget the name. That was natural too, perhaps.

After he had left, I rose and picked it up and stowed it away in the drawer where Sajjad's old letters were.

And now—on Doomsday—it is a relief to observe how shamefacedly the moment that gave birth to such a friendship, sadly passes me by, while the moment of its death does not.

The Seeds of Truth

When the Hindi critic, Namwar Singh, got the Akademi Award in 1972, his five-minute speech on the occasion was laudable. He launched into an attack on Hindi literature. Before undertaking to decorate his house, he said he had taken upon himself the job of clearing all the cobwebs from their nooks and corners.

This is as it should be. Still, after due deliberation, I should be inclined to think of it all as rather one-sided. Who can profess to assess from the other side the intensity of each moment one has lived through? If literature is a house of a kind, it does indeed have to be swept and dusted. But in the cleansing processes, the rubbish does not have to be deposited at the neighbour's door. And if in the enthusiasm to clean up, the brick and mortar of the building too are brought down, would that too form part of the critical job?

I have met Kulwant Singh Virk quite a few times. . . Yet I do not get the impression that he is involved in problems that a man of letters is usually confronted with. In June 1972, he had landed up at my house after a lapse of two years or so.

The atmosphere conjured up by Hindi literature is like the smoke that one associates with a coal fire. As references to it increased with the post-Independence years, names became more meaningful. Yet, when the variable winds had settled, instead of a clear flame, sparks of rivalries began shooting forth.

Courses prescribed in schools and colleges were tampered with by those who had the pull, and many a page was consequently being blackened by the distortion of certain images . . .

Virk touched on the subject in dismay. 'But this sort of thing doesn't happen anywhere in the world. Why should it in Punjabi . . .'

Just as children cannot determine parentage, so one cannot the language one is born to. And if this was the shape things were taking in Punjabi, well, there was not much one could do . . .

It was rather late in the day to think of writing in another language, no matter what anyone said about it . . .

Virk asked me: 'Whether you've written ill or well, tell me, does it matter to anyone?'

That was a question I had constantly put to myself. If no one had benefited from my stories or poems, so what? I did not expect any recognition for my work. And the years wasted on them had been my own. Why, in the name of sanity, had my contemporaries got into this kind of fending as if I had been responsible for wasting their lifetimes.

Virk went on probing to get some reaction from me. I avoided direct answers and showed him the new novella I had written—*Ak da Boota*. I was trying to show him this way, that there was no point in his losing his cool either. I explained that the plant *ak* was symbolic really of the bitter truth I sought to enlarge in the book. Some of the near relatives of the heroine contrived to kill her. Her brother got tired of the search for

the culprit. Though faces are drawn from fear, lips remain
sealed in both the villages: the one of her parents, the other of
her in-laws, as though they were all suffering from epilepsy.
Someone suggests a remedy. 'The snuff they prescribe for
patients suffering from this disease is made from the milky
juice of the *ak*. What if I stuff some of the same snuff up the
nostrils of both the villages . . .?'

Virk was highly amused. 'You must have seen the plant, I
guess . . . but do you know how it is propagated?'

'I only know that no one's ever sown any seed, yet you
find *ak* growing wild all over.'

'You've seen fluff flying out from the plant, haven't you?'
I nodded my head.

'Well, in every bit of fluff is hidden a teeny-weeny winged
seed . . . and wherever it flies and falls, a plant sprouts . . .'

'That's as wonderful as the truth, isn't it? No one plants the
seed of truth anywhere, yet it has wings. Wherever it flies and
falls, it grows . . . Or else no farmer would ever have harvested
a true acre.' My mind regained its tranquility. By the next post
the day following came a copy of *Soviet Literatures* which was
a special number on Indo-Russian literature. An article by the
Russian poetess, Rimma Kazakova, on a book of mine that had
been translated into Russian, ended with the lines:

> *She cannot but esteem this courage—to share with another*
> *one's most treasured and painful experience, and thereby to*
> *become a friend, mentor and comrade-in-arms.*

Warm ashes of pain, which have burnt out and become strength, are generously offered to Russian readers from the gentle but firm hands of a remarkable woman of faraway Punjab. She may be sure that thousands of hands are stretched out to meet hers.

How could I have missed Rimma? I have been to Moscow four times. How could I not have met her? Howsoever that be, in this moment of complete isolation, I feel our hands are clasped . . .

One never knows to which corners of the earth these winged *ak* seeds fly . . .

I had imagined having seen the wings of fairies in folktales, and now I have seen for myself on the good earth, the seeds of compassion taking on wings and flying and falling and sprouting.

A Certain Silence

My poetry does not fit into the pattern of any of the usual *Kavi Darbars*. That is why I do not take much interest in these poetry recitation sessions. When Professor Pritam Singhji was the principal of Government College, Ludhiana, he put a question to the School Board at one of its meetings: 'Why are the editors of anthologies usually not the writers themselves?' Economically too, he implied, the writers therefore stood to lose. Eventually, although the total amount involved was cut down to less than half (from ₹5000 to ₹2000 to be precise) it was decided that the anthologies prescribed for course books for that year were to be edited by writers. Because of the esteem in which he held me, I responded to his invitation to the jubilee celebrations of the college. The time at my disposal was rather limited, and though I had to return by the first flight next morning, Professor Pritam Singhji came to see me off at the airport. When the plane landed we learnt that it was not a passenger plane at all; it was being used to carry products of the local mills. There were only a few seats and the rest of the plane was fully loaded with cargo. The Professor laughed. 'You'll have a lot of bundles for company.'

'I have done this all my life,' I said. 'I have had little human company of any sort.'

What deep truths are embedded in the simplest of words, I have often thought. This simple truth dawned on me with great force during a meeting at the government level called in 1972, to arrange the celebration of the first twenty-five years of Independence. After a protracted two-hour discussion on how the symposia were to be arranged, I observed:

> *Whether you think of poems, songs or plays—let's not lose sight of certain basic factors. Each one of us must subject himself to self-criticism; secondly, let's be clear on the role of litterateurs in shaping things to come; thirdly, let those guiding the ship of state not forget that they too must undergo a change of heart.*

A pall of silence fell on all my compeers assembled.

Yet, before anything should be said to those at the helm of affairs, what of the writers themselves?

I recall the post card I had received from a contemporary who had been allotted the task of compiling an anthology of short stories, including one of mine, for a certain course of study. 'You have my permission . . . only would you kindly indicate whether any payment would be made?'

The result was that the story was excluded from the anthology.

I also recall the incident when a certain set of books was put up to the University for approval, and a certain editor had not sought permission of any of the writers he had included. Some had protested mildly but the publishers had silenced them with a pittance. The protest I had lodged was on the basic principle that permission had formally to be obtained before any publication was undertaken. Thrashing out this 'basic principle' once and for all, a question was raised by one member of the Board. 'Will it make any basic difference to the book if Amrita Pritam's poem is thrown out?' The decision of the Board was that, indeed, it would not!

Bemused, I said to myself, there are imperfections everywhere. Can these boards be flawless? Will they one day pass a dictum—'To hell with the names . . . throw out all the poems! Will it make the slightest difference, what is in or out?'

Light-heartedly, I switch on the radio. By a strange coincidence, someone is singing a *ghazal* by Ahmed Nadeem Kazmi:

> *At the crack of dawn they go to bazaars*
> *With bundles of honesty on their heads . . .*

Silver Linings to Clouds

The darkest of clouds have silver linings. I therefore look skywards whenever I can with an eye of wonder . . .

In the course of translating an American novel, I came up against certain words I found in no dictionary. Harbans Singhji from the USIS sent me a dictionary to help me out. On the flyleaf he had written, 'To Amrita Pritam: with all the good words from this dictionary!' I was deeply touched. My contemporaries so far had mostly sought out the more abominable ones for me from wherever they could. Someone had now reversed the process. How had this come about? I was thrilled anyhow in the same way that I was thrilled by a telephone call during the Bangladesh war. The voice at the other end had said: 'I've come to Delhi just for a day from the front. Can I see you?' During his visit that evening, the *jawan* recounted the woes of Bengali refugee women. 'The overwhelming majority of them are old and decrepit though there are some pretty ones too. We row them across to the refugee camp . . . I wanted to tell you about the effect of your novels on those who read them. They dare not treat women with disrespect!' A sense of fulfilment came over me. Whatever I had written had at last reached where it should have. Whether it had found a place on the tables of learned critics or not, it had reached much further—to the hearts of common soldiers . . .

I am reminded of an earlier episode. A soldier had sent me his poems by registered post just before he had left for the war. 'Should I come back alive, I'll one day return to claim them.

Should I not, do please have them printed.' My eyes filled with tears for one whom I had neither seen nor met, but who had such implicit faith to entrust his manuscripts to me.

In June 1972, Dhuswan Swamy, Cultural Counsellor at the Nepalese Embassy, paid me a visit. He had jotted down in his diary: 'When I read Amrita Pritam, my anti-Indian feeling vanished.'

'*My pen has broken traditional rigidities, there where my love has taken me!*' This poem was written in the mountains in the border regions during the 1960 war; but one climbs other heights when one builds bridges of love with people of other lands . . . and at these bridges the only thought is one of silent gratitude to all who have helped me be where I am . . .

Patches of Sunshine

Till Partition, the one thing among all others I wanted preserved was a poem by Sahir, titled *Taj*. He had it framed and mounted before presenting it to me. Later he gradually added a great deal to my collection, which is by now a veritable treasure trove buried in the depths of my cupboard.

In that collection is a leaf I had brought from Tolstoy's grave and a round piece of paper, on one side of which is inscribed *Asian Writers Conference* and on the other, *Sahir Ludhianvi*. This was a conference badge. Sahir had removed his badge and pinned it on me and he had taken mine in exchange. That piece of paper is now lying by the side of the leaf from Tolstoy's grave. Is it a leaf from my own grave?

There also sits among these souvenirs an ashtray from Vietnam which was given to me at Baku in Azerbaijan by the poetess Mirwarad Khanum—with the words, 'When the moment of creativity comes to you—and that inner light blends with the smoke from your cigarette, think of me.'

With the years, faces have appeared and disappeared... not only those of others, but mine as well. In my eyes, my own face becomes real and alive only when I am in the act of writing a poem.

Father, I remember, had a shiny little brass casket in which was a bit of leather wrapped carefully in gossamer-like silk. This relic he had solicited and been given by those who claimed they had Guru Gobind Singh's shoes in their possession. Coming down through the years, all that remained of the shoes with these folk was some piece of leather you would not recognize was once a shoe. Father was always most reverential whenever he opened the drawer containing that shiny little brass casket. One never knows how and when and whose touch gives sanctity to something. I am only aware that certain things bring up memories which transform an ordinary human being into a state approaching divinity itself.

Among these priceless treasures are all Imroz's letters, a few from Sajjad, three or four from Sahir and some from both my children.

There are also some letters from my readers and some writers all over the world. There is an atlas from the Uzbek poetess, Zulfia; wine jars from the Georgian poet, Arak Ali

Abashidge; a pictorial carpet and modern profile of Gorky's from the Baku poet, Rasool Raza; perfumes, brooches and necklaces from the Bulgarian writers Bagriana, Dora Gabe, Stanks and Kaminova. There is also half a silver bracelet from Uleg, the director of the Bulgarian Theatre. This was part of her inheritance from her mother and presenting it to me she had said, 'By sharing this, we are sisters from now on.' A sculpture the Bulgarian artist, Antonia, made of me is among the same treasures.

Then there is the disc of the music of *White Nights* given by the Yugoslav, Grosdana, and the Georgian piece composed by Shalve Mashwelidze on the poem Arak Ali had written about me.

A sweater from Mori Moti, the Japanese writer, and a fan from the Chinese, a bronze cast of Tagore given to me on Tagore Day in Moscow, and a line that Faiz Ahmed Faiz had written on a book of mine: 'Can wounds be healed I know not—I only know lips are sealed . . .'

On my lips are words of gratitude for those friends far away, who spent so much of their precious time in translating my poems and stories into their languages.

Igor Serebriakov has placed me under an obligation by compiling a book of my selected poetry in Russian; Charles Brasch from New Zealand spent much of the time he was in India in translating a good many more; Iliana Cura translated a good few of my poems into Serbian and then again into Albanian; Grozdima Olujic has translated my stories and an abridged version of my novel *Pinjjar* and Mori Moti has translated some of my poems into Japanese. George Griffith arranged a whole evening in London for recitations from my poetry. Carlo Coppolo from Michigan devoted an entire number of his journal to my poems and stories; Pritish Nandi, the Indian poet, Mahendra Kulshreshta and Manmohan Singhji too, spared no pains in translating my poems into English. Khushwant Singh did one novel and Krishna Gorowara has done three, besides stories, articles, and so much more. These are patches of sunshine in the sky over me.

So many from my own country have given me so much of their affection and done me so much honour. I have had 15 books published in Urdu, three in Kannada, two in Gujarati, two in Marathi; two in Malayalam; and indeed all that I have written has appeared in Hindi also. It is these Hindi books which have given me economic stability. Ironically, I have no anthology of my selected works in Punjabi, the language I write in, but I do have one in Hindi. I was overwhelmed by the foreword written for it by Sumitranandan Pant. Dr Bhagwant Saran Upadhyaya also wrote an analytical appreciation of my contribution to the field of letters for eventual inclusion in his own collected works. I stand deeply indebted, in all humility, to such outstanding writers. In the number of the 1968-69 journal of Carlo Coppolo's I have already mentioned, the Hindi writer Revti Saran Sharma contributed a detailed assessment of my work under the caption *The Search for Feminine Integrity*.

Some other endearing letters are among my possessions. Principal Teja Singh, one of the few worthwhile critics in

Punjabi, in a letter dated March 23, 1950, offered me this consoling thought: 'Do not get throttled by newspaper reports. Your writings belong on the same shelves as classics. Do not take to heart the way they are cavilling at your poetry.'

I met Prabod Kumar Sanyal, the well-known Bengali writer, for the first time in Nepal in 1960. I was impressed by his profundity. On my return to Delhi, I read that great novel of his on which a film has been based; while he on his return to Calcutta went through my *Pinjjar.* He wrote what he thought of it in the correspondence that followed, but somehow he had mislaid my address when he was on a visit to Delhi. He had a faint idea that I lived in one of the newer colonies of the capital on the way to the Qutab Minar, and with that he began exploring until finally he ran me down in the broiling heat of a summer afternoon. He was wet with perspiration but his eyes twinkled with laughter as he greeted me: 'After all, I knew you lived somewhere in Delhi. At the most, I would have had to knock at a few more doors before finding you.' I was indeed touched by such affection.

A letter of February 2, 1958, from Xnan Dieu who lives in Hanoi:

> The Spring Festival (beginning with the traditional Vietnamese New Year) is approaching, and your Poetry Selection in the peach-blossom wrapper makes me feel as if spring has already come to me. Our President, Ho Chi Minh, is paying a visit to your great country soon. I believe you are one of the friends who will extend to him a most cordial welcome . . .

A letter of July 29, 1953, from D K Badekar to Prabhakar Machwe:

Pinjjar subjects the creative artist to a test in restraint. My only desire is that the Marathi reading public should have it in their hands. My friend Shri Joshi alone is capable of making it throb, like the original, in translation.

Prabhakar Machwe has always been a good friend. I have had many favours from him in his usual unostentatious way.

Jainendra Kumar was one of the first Hindi writers to praise my work in a letter written to a friend of his, who later passed it on to me. I cannot trace that letter now but I shall always remember how good a friend Jainendra Kumar has always been.

Charles Brasch, the late editor of *Landfall* and an established poet, wrote on March 9, 1964:

I have read The Skeleton (Pinjjar), and I want to tell you how deeply moved I was by it. You have created the story with beautiful feeling and fine economy and restraint. It is a work to be proud of.

Oddly enough, at the same time, I recall how many letters a contemporary sent to numerous papers and to the All India Radio urging them to knock my name off their records.

Going through many of these letters in Punjabi I get hot and cold all over.

3

ORDEAL BY FIRE

Create an idealized image of yourself and try to resemble it. These were the words with which Kazantzakis greeted his beloved the very first time he met her. I too had heard these words, not from anyone's lips, but through my own senses . . .

I kept repeating them . . . each and every time I thought I had bungled . . .

I am not quite sure that the words have brought about any magical transformation in me. What I am conscious of is that they have helped me. Perhaps the magic lies in this feeling one has to getting nearer the idealized self . . . and the world of my imagination becomes a more cheerful place.

I can only say that all my life, I have been making a sustained effort to live up to those words and the effort itself is like a prop, giving me courage, like when at eighteen I faced the moment of separation from my husband. I said to him: 'Deep down in your mind you have accepted that we must go our own ways. But you are worried about the supercilious looks and the wagging tongues when the news of the divorce is out. Let people witness our separation. After two days or ten, they will tire themselves out and they will be silent . . . Armed with the truth within us, we will brave their fulminations. We will come out unscathed from this ordeal of fire . . . and you will see yourself being cured of your eczema.'

And so in September 1963 we fixed the date when we would begin to live separately—January 8, 1964, to be precise. We stuck to it. The astonishing thing was that by February he had got rid of his eczema after 18 years! And without treatment of any kind!

As I sit back and review the past, I see that all we had needed was the courage to face the truth. Ultimately, it was this courage that gave us both moral and physical strength.

A similar situation had arisen in 1960. Not that there was room for any doubt about Imroz's love for me, yet somewhere deep down inside him was an inexplicable conflict. He was in a state of irresolution. He could not get at what he called the black man at the back. But our combined efforts finally established our victory. 'The black man' had disappeared. We had freed ourselves forever of unwanted manacles. It was at this time, however, that Imroz began to have continuous fever. X-rays were taken. But 'he' could not have been caught and exposed through X-rays. Another month had to go before 'he' surfaced on 'his' own. I am aware of the fact that the tears I shed were not commensurate with the vision I had of my idealized self. I was diminished at the time, diminished into a pigmy.

However it became more or less clear to me that unless Imroz went off to some place far away from me, his fever would not leave him.

Must one pass through desolate deserts to reach out to the oasis? Must the depth of the thirst within and the reason for it be measured first? No matter how difficult it was, when we took the sad step towards a temporary parting, miraculously enough, Imroz became normal.

We decided to part for three years. As a consequence, he was able to see me as I am and to realize that I was the only one he needed in this world.

The battle between him and his ailing self was won because of our conviction that we were never going to live our lives in half-truths. But if either of us felt we were not doing quite the right thing by this parting, we would always be free to retreat.

A question once put to me in the course of a television interview by Revti Saran Sharma comes to my mind. 'Amrita! If the heroines of your novels in search of truth leave their homes, don't you think the effect of it can be shattering—in the social context, I mean?' Pat came my reply, 'If false social values have until now accounted for broken homes, let a few more be broken—but, mark you from now on, at the altar of truth!'

I know how arduous a task it is to walk the path of truth. Yet if an idealized image of the self is created, in the endeavour to resemble it, one gets nearer the goal.

Truth one day, is proved false the next. Truth to me is honest thought that brings about harmony between the body and the mind . . . like in a well-tuned musical instrument.

Imroz

Love put its thumb impression
On the page of life.
But who'll settle the debt?

During an Urdu poetry recitation session, people flocked around Sahir for his autograph. When they drew back, I thrust the palm of my right hand out for an autograph. With his pen Sahir spread ink on his thumb and pressed it to my outstretched palm, like unlettered folks do who cannot sign their names.

Neither he nor I could read this quaint autograph. But perhaps Sahir was responding to my own romantic imagination. With Imroz, on the other hand, barring the few earlier years, I have reached the region of ecstasy. Some measure of this ecstasy was a casual remark of his. A house guest one day got down to reading our palms. Of mine he observed, 'The line of wealth is deep and unbroken . . . you'll never be in want.' Imroz's was a different case altogether. 'You'll never be able to save anything . . . your line is all in bits . . .' Upon that Imroz clasped my hand in his and quipped: 'Never mind . . . we'll manage to hang together on one line!'

In 1964, when he pulled himself out of Patel Nagar to strike root at Hauz Khas, he had barely a hundred odd rupees with him after paying the servant's bill. Yet he had not a care in the world. He had his job in an advertising firm which brought him ₹1200 or so. He used to say: 'If only I had ₹10,000, I'd chuck this job and do what I have always wanted to.' Prices were steadily on the rise, but I did not have the heart to let him feel the pinch. Imroz had also to work at night which brought him another ₹500 a month. I was bent on saving that ₹10,000 he needed no matter how I tightened the housekeeping budget.

I had just about hit the target in a little over a year when without a note of warning, he quit work. The other income of ₹500 also came to an abrupt end. I was at the time scheduled to go on a three-month visit to Europe. In my absence, he began experimenting with the latest craze in batik-printed garments and rushed his brother all the way to the South to ferret out a wizard in the field.

By the time I had returned, a place had been rented at ₹300 per month in Green Park, where two hired men had begun to grapple with the complexities of batik. There were huge cauldrons in which different colours were being boiled for bales of newly purchased cloth. The colours did not come out evenly and the masses of messy cloth were doused again and again in the cauldrons in the effort to give them the authentic colour. They were put out a line, then dripdropping, to dry. All this was only the beginning of the batik mystique.

Imroz in those days was like the Delhi weather that brought out blisters in the body with the heat of the afternoon and made it shrivel and shrink with the cold at fall of night. It was futile, my commenting on the situation.

To add to the problems, Imroz's master tailor went snip-snap, snip-snap with his scissors through the best of the finished batik. What came out were shirts with waists suitable for the classic figure of the beloved in Urdu poetry . . .

About 500 of these shirts were dumped here and there. There were no buyers for them and they were wasting storage space. A full-sized cupboard and a huge trunk had to be acquired and between us we hastily shut the doors of the first and clamped down the lid of the second and got them out of sight with some relief.

We almost had a buyer for the shirts one day. An American woman took a fancy to them. Alas, she insisted on trying one out on her own body which was not exactly the Urdu poet's idea of the form of his beloved. How she managed to get inside that shirt I do not know. But presently, she screamed for help. She was having trouble wriggling herself out of it. 'Pl-e-e-ase get me out of this!'

The ten thousand rupees had gone and there were debts to pay. Imroz sold off the only piece of land he possessed for ₹6,500. With some payments which were due to him for certain book-jacket designs he had done, the batik experiment had made a dent of ₹20,000 in our total budget.

All there was to show for it was a silk shirt and *sari* he had himself laboured on, as a gift for me. I think of that ₹20,000 every time I wear that shirt or *sari*. The episode still saddens me sometimes, but Imroz laughs it off. He tells me, 'No empress in the history of this big wide world can have draped herself in as expensive a garment as that *sari* of yours! You should be the happiest woman alive at the thought of being so unique!' Unique indeed to have in my wardrobe a shirt and a *sari* worth ₹20,000!

Who can be richer than me? I am richer for the wealth of his courage which will laugh at a loss of ₹20,000—a sum of money he has never had before or since.

Imroz is an easy man to get to know. His is a creative mind. He is full of ideas which he expresses through a variety of media—paper, canvas, wood, and so forth. But it is beyond him to rein in his energies to create a great work of art.

He did wonders in textile designing. I always used to think whenever I saw his work-sheets, what wonderful materials these could make. To design on paper was well within his power. But to transfer the paper work on to cloth was in the power only of mill owners. And those who own the mills do not have the eyes to see the beauty of his designs. Our experience of the mill owners who came over to see his designs can be described in two words of Ayn Rand. They were 'perfect idiots'.

The most compelling reason for Imroz to turn to his batik experiment, as I see now, was that he wanted to be free of any kind of subservience to the tastes of mill owners. Of course, so long as the garment trade was in the hands of hired men, it was not picking up; but when Imroz took to doing it all on his own, each item he executed bore the unique stamp of his individuality. Alas! as for buyers, but for the occasional Japanese and Americans, no one fancied his work.

Batik having failed as a means of livelihood, the entire setup was wound up. Imroz's mind turned to other things. He began designing dials for watches and clocks. This did not call for a big investment, ₹50 or so was enough. Whenever he managed to save up that much he would dash out, buy a time-piece and get down to the job straight away. We have one cupboard which is full of this phase of his experiments. There are so many watches and clocks that it is simply not possible to wind all of them daily. Sometimes when we are in the mood, we bring out the whole lot of them and have a session at winding them and then sit back to listen to the litany of tick-tocks.

Watches are expected to run to the same time. Imroz's mind ticked on two sets of time: one, the common time that everyone abides by; the other the time frozen by the poets in their most significant lines. He would thus remove the dials which tell merely the time of the day, and put in their place dials inscribed with verses from Faiz, Kazmi, Waris Shah, Shiv Kumar, and so on.

In the same way, he worked on designs for calendars. They came in all shapes. There was one designed like a chessboard with the days and dates pictorially represented to suit his fancy. If a month was indicated with a castle, the days were green leaves; another month was a musical instrument, with keys and strings to represent the days.

The country would have stood to gain if there were exhibitions of such articles of craft. But neither Imroz nor I can assume to have the power to order these things.

When one decides to belong to another's present, his time past also is contained in time-common-to-both as it ticks on in weal or woe. Separateness in terms of time is then unthinkable. In the general course of things, no one can be treated in isolation, whether or not one has seen the other. Each is a part of the other because of this continuous common-time factor or, if this is to be believed, because of the law of the transmigration of souls that governs all.

Imroz is aware of the regard I have for Mohan Singhji. So when he got down to designing the jacket of his book *Jandre,* instead of illustrating the title of the first poem with two locks, symbolizing my children, who, according to Mohan Singh were locks really to two flowers, Imroz drew three. 'Mohan Singh hadn't the eyes to see you—the biggest of the lock. That makes it three, doesn't it?' Imroz had really got to the back of my mind . . .

Imroz knows also how much love I bore for Sahir. Completing his design for the jacket of Sahir's book *Aao Koi KhwabBunain* , he came to where I was sitting with Davinder, sketch-paper in hand. Davinder, incidentally, is the only other friend with whom I can talk without any inhibitions whatsoever, about Sahir. He, therefore, tried to dig into the past, took one look at the title, another at me—but Imroz it was who fathomed my past. 'The moron's still at weaving dreams. Couldn't he ever think of giving them some shape?' I laughed. 'The weaver is indeed a moron if he still does not realize . . .' The three of us had a good laugh.

I am a trifle perplexed, however. To what extent has Imroz got me really if he has me with the pain that dilutes his own share of happiness?

Upon that I once said to him, 'Imroz! If I had got Sahir, I wouldn't have got you!'

Quick came the reply, 'I certainly would've got you even if I'd had to pull you out from his house . . .'

Had Imroz not been what he is, I could never have written:

No relationship with man,
Not one word—father, brother, friend, husband
Could have described you . . .
Each of these words now gain in depth.

I have written many letters to Imroz. One that I feel deeply still, was written in August 1967 from Dubrovnik in the south of Yugoslavia:

My friend

Far beyond the extremity of anxiety-ridden realities is something called *fantasy;* that I think is found after a patient, long search beyond even the commonly imagined periphery of fantasy. That is where you come in. In the words of Henry Miller, all art will one day have come to a dead end, but the artist alone will go on when life will be art itself. If it is assumed that this imaginatively conceived world of Miller's is a reality, say a thousand years from now, I'll say only this: it was your fault you came into existence one thousand years too early! . . . the relationship with you is of incalculable value. Or shall I put it in this way—each one of us exists in the past. How can I evaluate you since your roots shoot out only into the future? Could I buy a copy of a paper from a newsagent a thousand years from now, I might perhaps then be able to follow how exactly your contribution to the realm of art has been assessed.

I will not attach 'perfection' to you since it gives me the shuddering feeling of something cold and solid to which nothing can be added and from which nothing can be taken away. But you have the power to overcome decay, and to go on creating. 'Perfection' is the concept I attach to the picture of Christ I see before me in this church. It leaves me speechless. With you one can speak with ease . . . as if the very breath of my existence emanated from you . . . O breath of my life . . .!

As I sit writing to you from this foreign country, it occurs to me that it is the 15th today: the day of our country's Independence. Could one give a personality to this day, I would say you are the 15th of August for me, since with you came the emancipation of the being that is me . . .

A Concatenation of Events

I wrote an article in the February 5, 1972 number of *Status* that went:

In a Rumanian poem, a poet goes and borrows chairs from the houses in the neighbourhood and arranges them as it were in a Hall of Audience. And he recites his poems to the empty seats. They are his best listeners. So he thinks, since they do not make any show of enthusiasm nor subject themselves to the voice of the censor. And how does the tramontane wind blow in our country? A whole band of self-seeking authors keeps waddling after chairs. Their ultimate goal seems to become 'cultural furniture' so to say, in the Conference Rooms of Establishments.

The last few lines in the next para of the article were more definitive:

Any author worth his name must surely wish to go coursing down centuries through the arteries of his readers: manifesting their dreams and illumining the dark corners of their lives.

There was a reason for the note of sadness in what I wrote. A certain writer had secured some support from the Sahitya Academi Award Committee. I had gone through his book as conscientiously as I could, but could not in all fairness to the author and to Punjabi literature, bring myself to cast a vote in his favour. On discovering this, the man made a beeline for Chandigarh, and scathingly attacked my work in a couple of papers. He petulantly described my novels as *novelchoos* and accused me of plagiarism in my poems. Towards the middle of that year—at the end of July to be precise—his sense of revenge took a more vulgar form. Holding a glass of liquor high in the air he danced a jig at the house of another contemporary and jubilantly proclaimed; 'I've got her . . . I've got her . . . for three years! I've been elected to the Bharatiya Jnanpith Committee for three years. I'll lay a wager . . . The Award won't go to her during this tenure of mine.'

Another of his cronies joined in. 'We've got her . . . We've got her for five years!' And he informed the revellers: 'Amrita would be completing her term as a member of the Sahitya Academi Executive this year. She can't have another term under the rules. We'll see that this road too is blocked for her . . .!'

Had I been present, I would have congratulated them on their make-believe election to the Akademi and the Jnanpith Committee but only Mohan Singh was there, looking mournfully on at this juvenile performance. He reported everything to me the following morning, word for word.

I shall not be there to see their wild sword-dances in the blinding light surrounding their awards and honours! My only desire is to penetrate deep into the hearts and souls of my readers. To whatever extent that has been possible, I have reached somewhere . . .

Towards the end of the year, I had more experiences of a similar nature. There was a call from Chandigarh.

'For which book would you be casting your vote?'
'To the one I think merits the award . . .'
'How about the one on Lenin?'
'That's hardly a book . . .'

'True. But the author's getting old. He ought to be given it.' Then he sought my view on what I considered the outstanding work in the field.

I told him my vote would go to *Tin Rattan.* I thought there was something fresh about the way the past had been recalled in the first part of the book, and there was a remarkable relevance to the present in the second half. I heard the click of the telephone as it was replaced at the other end.

I later heard that two more opinions were still to be obtained and that these would be manoeuvred so as to nullify mine.

Opinions can differ on the merits of a work. But how often are judgements in these matters passed upon merit?

On January 1, 1973, I was released from having to serve on the Executive of the Sahitya Academi after a period of five years. It is perhaps not the done thing to feel relieved in being cast out from a position of responsibility, yet I confess, that is precisely how I felt.

Whenever during that period someone talked to me to put in a word for so-and-so on such-and-such lines, I used to share my amused reactions with Imroz. 'Why don't you hammer into their heads once and for all that you are not going to be put through this five-year stint?' During the last year of my term, particularly, the 'putting-in-of-a-word' got worse till there was a message attended by a threat' that if so-and-so did not get the award, I would have to face indictments through newspapers.

This went on all the time. Whenever word goes round that I am compiling an anthology of Punjabi poems or short stories, threats are directed at me: 'If you omit such-and-such poem or such-and-such story, beware of a Special Number that'll be brought out against you . . .' A Special Number! What next? However, I have got used to such attacks . . .

My contemporaries labour under the illusion that TV programmes are chalked out in consultation with me. They telephone to ask for a TV review or recitation of their poems. In vain do I plead with them and explain that I am not in the least connected with programming. To no effect. They go off and write a couple of columns in the papers or address letters to Ministers . . .

Some of them are off on a new track. They have branded my work as pornographic. After I had been elected Chairperson of the Reception Committee of the 1970 Asian Writers' Conference, this campaign became more insistent. As a result, a screening committee was appointed to go through my work to find out whether there was anything in it which could sustain the accusation. The verdict was that the poems I had written in 1968 on Czechoslovakia were pornographic.

This definition of pornography is unique in the history of the literatures of the world.

Newspapers' Cock-'n-bull Stories

On May 15, 1973, the University of Delhi conferred the D.Litt. degree on me, *honoris causa*. Each of us so honoured said a few

words befitting the occasion. So did I. The following morning
The Times of India cooked up the most fantastic story for its
readers: Subbulakshmi and I, the report went, leapt high in the
air for joy! I reproduce word for word what I said . . . not that
it is called for, but because of what was said at the time in the
newspapers.

> I began with a few lines from a poem I wrote some time ago:

> *There was a hamlet hewn of stone*
> *From the Sun and Moon Dynasties*
> *They lived there*
> *And they said:*
> *The mortar and pestle were ordained*
> *By the fates to live there*
> *Till they ate forbidden fruit . . .*

> *From the stones rubbed together*
> *I rose as Fire in the heat of summer.*
> *Wherever the babbling brooks took me–*
> *Hot embers were smeared all over me*
> *And the hot winds blew about*

> *And raced and chased me*
> *And placed words in my hand*
> *With the injunction–*
> *'Don't mistake these for black wriggle-squiggles*
> *These criss-cross lines will contain your fires.'*
> *And the wind flew ahead and blew the words:*
> *'May your life afire*
> *Be shared by them . . . the words!'*

If I have desired anything in my life, it is that these
words catch fire from the breath of my being. You from Delhi

University have comprehended the value of these words; have been seized of the fire in these words. For the recognition of that fire, do I thank you all.

The Battle of Dharma

The greatest moment in the *Mahabharata* for me is when the battle between the Kauravas and the Pandavas is about to begin, and Yudhishter walks down the field unescorted for the traditional leave-taking from friends and relatives assembled in the enemy's camp across.

Spotting Bhishma Pitamah in their midst, he goes up to him, and dutifully offers his salutations . 'I am having to fight against you, kindly accord your permission and bestow your blessings on me so I emerge victorious.'

Bhishma answers, 'My physical self must be on the side of Duryodhana because I have eaten his salt, but bound by the law of dharma, my mind will be with you, my chief concern will be your well-being and success.' In the same manner, Yudhishter goes up to his *gurus,* Dronacharya and Kirpacharya.

I have had to fight a lifelong battle with my contemporaries. Only now that I am constrained to write about it, I appeal to them in the name of truth not to subtract anything or make excuses.

The *Mahabharata* scene continues. Yudhishter stands in the centre of the field and proclaims: 'I stand here to welcome the valiant who will stand forth and fight on my side.' Hearing this, Duryodhana's younger brother, Yuyutas, steps out from the ranks.

History repeats itself. I repeat the same words to welcome budding young writers . . .

The battle is bound to go on and on all my life . . . and ever after . . . so that not only this generation, but the generations to come writing from a sense of truth, will be welcomed by time itself.

I always thought of Sant Singh Sekhon as an honest literary critic. As the years went by, my assessment of him found more justification. I regarded Mohan Singhji as a good poet and a man with a good though weak heart. My early judgement of him was of a man who would not stick to his guns over values and principles. This has turned out to be correct. On the other hand, Navtej Singh and Kartar Singh Duggal have not merited the praise expressed in my articles *Mera Humdum Mera Dost* and *Thanda Dastana*. I had written the first article in good faith and the second with some hope, but alas! both my faith and hope were belied.

I had some expectations from Harbhajan Singh. Some, not much. I was neither dismayed nor surprised when he got his henchmen to indulge in all the mudslinging. I felt rather sad that a poet should so sully the spring of his own creativity . . .

For others like Sadhu Singh and Hamdard, who are crippled and cramped by their narrow-mindedness, I have neither faith nor hope. I turned my back on Gurbachan Singh Bhullar when

I saw the story he concocted about Harbhajan Singh and me for the May 1973 number of *Preetlari.*

Among the letters of congratulation I received from friends and fans when Delhi University conferred on me the D.Litt. degree, there came one from Gurbaksh Singh.

In my younger years, I had not only deep regard for him but also held him as an ideal for emulation. I had also assumed that with the wisdom and weight of his years he would stand fast by principles and lend me a helping hand through the turns and twists of life. Instead, he decided pretty early to retreat into his own world. Just as well. Sooner or later I had to learn to stand and walk alone. I had no grievance with Gurbaksh Singh and my respect for him was never dimmed. On reading in his autobiography a few good lines about me, I promptly wrote back, 'To me your lines are like a robe of honour.' He sent me a cordial reply.

When the story that I have referred to earlier appeared in *Preetlari,* Imroz said, 'It's quite possible Navtej Singh did the editing entirely on his own and Gurbaksh Singhji hadn't the chance to read it until after the mischief had been done.' He immediately sat down to address a letter to Sardar Gurbaksh Singh:

On going through the May number of Preetlari, I was astonished to see a story like 'Kasvati'. Not only was it downright slovenly as a creative piece but the angle from which it was written is equally condemnatory; not only is it false through and through, but the falseness shows so obviously that it can have no effect on Amrita. Surely what a paper prints, affects the reputation of the editors. There are, of course, innumerable papers in Punjabi that do discredit to the written word by printing rubbish. But, apparently, as you did not go through the scandalous story before it went to the press, you have done both us and yourself a great wrong. You have, in fact, placed *Preetlari* in the same category as the other purveyors of dirt that pass for papers.

I am a complainant at your door but my respect for you still abides.

As it happened, Imroz had arranged to go to Connaught Place at 6.30 that evening to meet Avtar Jandialvi who had arrived from London. I was due to meet Jelani Bano from Hyderabad at Western Court at 7. We left together. Avtar Jandialvi was dead on time, and had brought Harbhajan Singh along. On his insistence we went to *The Ramble*. I was tired of our efforts at vague conversation over the coffee so I turned to Harbhajan Singh and said:

'*Preetlari* has an endearing story on you this time.'

'It's as much against you,' He chortled.

'That I take for granted. I've got pretty used to attacks by now.' And I took a look at him, signifying thereby that he too had had a hand in it.

He paused long for a reply. 'But what could have prompted Navtej to print it? It should have had some movement at least. What an infliction on the poor readers!'

'What a pity! Two men's pleasure—the writer's and the printer's that is—at the cost of all those poor readers!'

There was again a long pause before the cat leapt out of the bag. 'Not two, I make the third of the pleasure-seekers. Bhullar has sunk to the level of such stories.'

'I feel sorry for him because he had the proven capacity to write a fine story like *Upra Marad'*, I said. As we rose to go our different way, Imroz hit the nail on the head. 'So that's what Harbhajan's capable of! He has himself bared to us his inner self. Imagine getting malicious pleasure out of the undoing of a promising young writer! Has the man no heart . . . finishing off a fine artist that way?'

At that time in 1960 when I was in real mental agony over Imroz, I often thought of Father, who was no more in this world. Gurbaksh Singhji was like a father figure to me at the time and so I wrote to him: 'The person I called *Darji* is no longer alive. I address you today by the same dear name. Should you be good enough to come for a day or two, perhaps you can help me resolve the conflict in my mind.' 'Gurbaksh Singhji made no response to my earnest request. Notwithstanding, I pulled myself together and came through that hour of crisis. But the strong impact Gurbaksh Singhji had made on me in my childhood persisted and because of this I imagined a reply from him to Imroz's complaint:

Dear Imroz!

Despite the poor type of stories that have found their way into Preetlari, *I take note of the regard you have for me. As*

you surmised quite rightly, 1 had not read the story in its
manuscript form. Do you really and truly have faith in me?
Then let me give you this assurance: I would never have
published the thing had I gone through it.

Alas! The real one that came was very different.

For me, a writer must have firm faith in the values and
principles he sets before himself. I felt deeply pained at
Gurbaksh Singhji's lack of faith in his own pen, not so much
in the story that his paper carried.

He sent such a weak reply to Imroz, that I felt alarmed.
He had written, 'My advice to you is to re-read the story.'
And this, after the author had stated clearly, was against two
contemporaries. 'Should the editors have the courage, they can
go ahead and print it.' Well, they did have the courage, and they
printed it—as simple as that!

Having done all they had conspired to, they had now the
nerve to say that it was not directed against Amrita, and on top
of it, she was being advised to re-read it!

Is this how it should be? I do not know that this can happen
anywhere else except in the Punjabi press. News gets distorted
according to the writer's fancy. At the World Hindi Conference
held at Nagpur in January 1975, more than a hundred writers
from thirty countries took part. Along with the foreign delegates
honoured, were fifteen writers from fifteen different languages
of our country. I was chosen to receive the award for my
contribution to Punjabi literature. There was no possibility for
doubt on this score, but a contemporary was not satisfied and

he reported: 'You contrived to get this distinction because of your Hindi publications, that were at best mere translations. In concealing the fact that your original compositions were in Punjabi, you must be arraigned as a traitor to the cause of that language.'

The intriguing fact is that the person responsible for this piece of perversity is not only associated with the paper I refer to, but is also a professor in the University of Delhi. What must one expect of the common man when someone in a position such as that can be the source of such distorted statements?

Usually, the communist press behaves more responsibly. Nevertheless I recall one instance of frightful irresponsibility. I cannot conceive of any press anywhere in the world sinking to the level of the daily *Lok Lehar* of August 1, 1975. It charged that *Nagmani,* the monthly magazine I publish, was vulgar and sex-oriented and plain pornography. It went on to say that as a result of the kind of poems I had written after my return from Yugoslavia, I had not been able to get a wink of sleep for three successive nights! Could any press surpass that? Yet not a squeak came from anyone in protest!

When my heart is heavy with such filth and calumny against me all I simply do is write a poem. At one such moment, I wrote:

You, who leap at shadows must know
Hearts, in flames, do not bear shadows!

All those who live by the pen are to my mind closely related. I therefore seem to take the strength in the pen of Sati and Harbhajan as my own. But I feel sad at the same time, though I have broken myself away from them and their kind.

I was fully aware that they did not share my sense of community. Principles and values do not find a place in their minds. Yet I feel there is something common between them and me and between all those anywhere in the world who live by the pen . . . And that includes my past, my present, as well as my future. It could be true of anyone thousands of years ago or with anyone in as many years' time in the future . . .

Seen, Heard and Experienced

Incidents one has witnessed, heard, or gone through, sometimes find their way through the conscious self into creative work. At others they get submerged in the labyrinthine subconscious, and yet surprisingly, without your realizing it, the subconscious influences your imaginative concepts.

4

IN SILENCE PASSION SMOTE

I was very young when I met Tagore. I had begun writing, but
as may be obvious, mainly juvenilia. He cajoled me into reciting
a poem—which I did rather coyly. The intent hearing I got was
not because I deserved it but because of the humanism that
glowed in him. This left a lasting impression on me. So when his
centenary was due to be celebrated in 1961, I felt the deep urge
to write a poem on him. The few lines I had got out of myself
were giving me scant satisfaction. I was to go to Moscow at
about this time. Mayakovsky's statue stood right opposite the
hotel in Gorky Street where I was staying. At about ten one night
when I opened my window, I saw a cluster of people around
the statue. Asking for the reason, I was told that young poets
often gathered there at night—either to read selections from
Mayakovsky's poetry or their own. Often passers-by stopped
and listened and at times asked for their favourite verses to be
recited. The session could last well into the early hours of the
morning. When the winds grew cold, they turned up the collars

of their coats; when it rained they held umbrellas over their heads. I too could not resist the temptation of slipping on my coat and joining the gathering. Not that I understood a word of Russian, but I felt the warmth of the language penetrate my being. In deep meditation I returned to my room feeling deeply the presence of Mayakovsky, of Gorky, and of Tagore . . . and I was suddenly seized with the compulsion to complete the poem on Tagore I had begun earlier.

The main character in the novella, *Ak da Boota*, is propelled by an unseen power to go to the railway station every evening at twilight, in search of his lost sister. He looks into the faces of the passengers in compartment after compartment of the incoming trains, until an even greater force pushes him into one of the trains going past his village. It is bitterly cold. He has nothing warm on him. He sits crouched through the long wintry night. He manages somehow to sleep a little, but is woken up rudely when the train screeches to a halt. And he is amazed to find that an aged man sitting by his side has shared with him his quilt.

A sudden flashback on this portion of the novel reminded me of my own plight four years earlier. I was travelling by the night train from Rumania to Bulgaria. I had on a light coat which was hardly a help in the freezing cold. I could not recall exactly when, but I felt a comforting warmth wrapping me up into deep sound sleep for the rest of the night. When I woke up in the morning, I discovered that the Bulgarian sitting by my side had tenderly covered me with his own overcoat.

I do not remember consciously putting this into the work I am speaking of, when I re-read it later. But I did have the feeling that the warmth of the night on that train was something I was to keep with me in reserve.

I wrote *Yatri* in 1968. While Sunderan came entirely out of the imagination, I knew the life-story of the titular character well enough to have written about him earlier. I knew the hero— from the day he was presented as an offering at the habitation of the *sadhus*. Although that was years ago, his sharply-chiselled dark face, with its sorrowful expression, comes clearly before my mind's eye even today. And even though the matrix of Sunderan was of my imagination, I had tears in my eyes when I came to write about her.

After completing the novella, when I began reading it out to Imroz, a lump came into my throat on the mere mention of her name. Again when I was listening to the translated version in Hindi in 1969 and later, correcting the proofs of the reprinted editions in Punjabi in 1971, a sort of restlessness came over me.

I could not understand this until the year 1973, when *Yatri* was being rendered into English. I felt then as though I was feeling my own pulse . . .

Bits and pieces of a writer's life always creep into novels and stories. The reverse happens in the case of Sunderan. She leaps at me from the pages of the book. Suddenly a kind of lamp lights up to dispel the pervasive darkness, to reveal that she is me.

I had not consciously transmuted my own being into hers and so for years could not quite place her in the realm of my own creation. The thing kept gnawing at my inner self, and even when I tried to come to grips with it, I could not recognize it quite clearly. When finally I did, I caught on to what was going on in my thoughts.

When Sunderan empties a basket of flowers at the feet of Shiva and Parvati, and pays obeisance to them, she gropes beneath the heap of flowers so that she can stealthily touch the feet of the one she loves standing by the statue being worshipped. I too had for years fixed my gaze on one face and shed tears as copious as those flowers from under which I yearned to stretch my hand out stealthily to touch him . . . in such a manner that no bystander would see or know.

For a long time Sunderan quietly keeps picking flowers and unseen, unobserved, touching the feet of the one she loves. For as long a stretch of time, it seems, I kept putting words together, stealthily touching the form in my imagination of the one I loved . . .

Although he whom Sunderan loved is there in flesh and blood, he is more like a glacially cold stone statue until the heat of her passion melts him. In a similar way, the intensity of my passion did not carry to the one I loved. For years I too stood at the place she did. It smote the stone—like silence and the flickering sparks were flung back at me.

Sunderan wears the necklace and nose-ring worn at the time of marriage, and when she comes to offer her obeisance to the one she worships and loves, for the last time, her tears settle on the fine gold thread of the nose-ring: as if the ornament itself had eyes welling up with tears . . .

O Lord! Will you never reveal the secret behind this hide-and-seek game that the subconscious keeps playing with the conscious?

I was not exactly eleven years old when Mother died. I have the last day of her life clear in my mind. I remember having stood the way Jagdeep, a character in *Ik Savaal,* stands beside his dying mother's bed.

And like Jagdeep, since I had prayed with all my heart and soul, 'Please do not take Ma away . . .' I was fully confident she would not be taken away. God heeded a child's prayers, did He not . . .? But Mother died. Like Jagdeep, I lost my trust in God.

And just as Jagdeep hides the *chappatis* made by his mother, 'I'll eat these bit by bit . . . day after day . . .' I too carefully crushed the dried up *chappatis* and preserved them in a box for as long as I could . . .

Of course, this part was consciously woven into the novella. But I do not think my father was a model for any facet of Mahant Kirpa Sagar in *Yatri.* It was only after his death, when the hero keeps on hearing echoes of his voice, that I felt the presence of Father and his voice:

> His voice had a liquid quality to it . . . more like the water of the stream . . . so that even when it came forth slowly, it had a certain depth to it and also a force within that made

it flow. Stone, leaf or dirt . . . anything thrown in would be carried away by the stream . . . or else the water would flow as over feet steeped deeply in . . .

The line 'without a friend, bereft of help have I been for ages now' that Mahant Kirpa Sagar chants again and again, I remember Father often reciting . . . His temperament was like Father's too. But for the quite conscious delineation of his character, I owe a good deal really to a *sadhu* friend of his.

When I turned home after the convocation ceremony at the University, Davinder shoved something into the pocket of his shirt. 'Didi!' he stuttered, 'I must be . . . er . . . permitted . . . I feel like performing a ceremony too. May I? You won't get angry? Say you won't.'

'Whatever's on your mind?' I laughed, 'Must be something good.'

He pulled out the silk handkerchief he had been hard at concealing. In a neat knot he had packed some cardamoms, candy, and the traditional sum of ₹21. 'Had your father been alive today . . . had you a brother . . . such a thanksgiving would have come from them . . . Do accept . . . as from one of them!'

My eyes filled with tears, and I was reminded of an incident from *Ik Savaal*. After the death of his old father, the hero gives away his young stepmother to the young man of her choice. Later, she has him over for dinner and says to him: 'Come, let mother and son eat from the same plate.' But before he starts eating he wants to know: 'Tell me first . . . are you mother, sister, or daughter to me?'

When I wrote this, Davinder featured nowhere in the picture. After fourteen years, when he offered me the silk handkerchief, the words came to my lips again, 'Tell me first . . . are you father, brother, or son to me?'

There is a story I wrote in the beginning of the year 1974. I cannot say what I was thinking of at the time. In the background is a temple on Swambhu Peak in Nepal to which a young girl, Rajshree, goes at the crack of dawn. She picks her way down to Beseega Stream where a couple of centuries earlier, sacrificial maiden of the same dynasty, a *kumari* that is, had committed suicide.

The lovelorn Rajshree often thinks of ending her life in the same way. As the story moves on, an age turns over in the heroine's mind. She stands face to face with her own self. And she begins to realize that what truth is at one time need not necessarily be truth at another. She turns away from death to the path of life.

Two years had passed by. I had not associated the character of Rajshree with any part of myself until one night when my sleep was interrupted. I found myself going back thirty-five years. I was barely twenty when I went to Gujranwala, to the same small house in the same narrow street where Father's sister Hakko died during the period of her forty day's penitential fast.

The same voice of Jeewi Bhagatni greeted my ears across thirty-five years. Good heavens . . . It's you I'm seeing, is it!' And as she had looked startlingly at me then, so she did now, with the palm of her hand pressing her lips. But it was Hakko herself I was being greeted by now.

The only woman alive whom I knew could have said that.

Jeewi . . . I looked into a mirror . . . and lo and behold! I discovered a distinct resemblance to my aunt . . . I saw through nature's own design in letting me into this secret. Or was it the shadow of events to come? I had been married. My mind was ill at ease. Seeing Hakko in myself, I began to cry as if with a foreboding of a similar end.

That was the time when I turned away from my death wish to a yearning for life . . . In heart-breaking pain, I asked why my feet had to tread that same trodden path. I was not going to die like Hakko; I was going to live my life out. This cycle of life and death was a mystery to me but even if what Jeewi Bhagatni said about my being Hakko in my previous life was true, I was not going to die like her in this one.

Yet this story was not consciously in my mind when I wrote about Rajshree in 1974.

One thing becomes increasingly clear with the passage of time. Many incidents form a part of the creative inspiration within days of their happening, while others may lie buried for years before they also become a part of the creative processes.

I can recall another incident similar to the one just described. I was in Nepal in 1960. For five successive evenings there were poetry-reading sessions. I was with some of the Nepali poets I had met earlier. One of them was relatively young and rather reserved. I had noticed that he would ask me every day to repeat a short poem of mine. When I was being seen off at the airport, he had come along with the others. It so happened that the plane was an hour late. During the waiting, he carried a heavy coat of mine for me. And when I was finally about to leave, he handed me my coat and whispered, 'Take the weight you can see with you. What you can't, is what I'll continue to carry!'

I was startled. On my return to Delhi, I wrote the story *Hungara.* It was not about him, but what he said had somehow found its way into it.

Do Aurtan is an example of a happening that took many years to come alive again. One of the two women of the title is the Shah's wife, while the other is his kept mistress.

Much that went into the story I had witnessed when I lived in Lahore. The traditional musical evening had been arranged on the occasion of the Shah's son's marriage. I had some acquaintance with the family, so when I learnt that the celebrated nightingale, Tamancha Jan, was to perform, I did not want to miss the opportunity of seeing and hearing her. And what an atmosphere there was around her! With a sweeping swagger she sailed in. The lady of the house turned green with envy, seeing her slender form enrapture the audience. Yet she could say nothing unseemly. After Tamancha Jan had sung, the bridegroom's mother took out a hundred-rupee note for payment from the fold of her veil. Tamancha felt insulted, but restrained herself. 'Keep it. After all, it is not the first time I've eaten from the Shah's house.' And so, aligning herself with the Shah, she humiliated the Shahani. The latter looked crushed for a fleeting moment, but regained her composure soon enough. With the note still held out, she thrust back, 'From the Shah, yes . . . but when will you ever take anything again from my hands?'

This was a strange encounter between two women. Against the social values of the time, it took on layer upon layer of meaning. Although Tamancha was a young, frail and comely woman, and the Shahani an ageing and overblown one, with a rather homely face and form, her pride in being a wife and mother could not be weighed down by all the beauty and charm that gold could buy.

This took me a good quarter century to weave into a story.

In 1975, when the film Kadambari based on my *Dharti, Sagar te Sippiyan* was on the sets, the director wanted me to write a song for the episode which deals with Chetna, who has waved all social acceptance aside and is totally involved with her love. When I attempted the exercise, spontaneously, the lyric I had written on my first meeting with Imroz in 1960 came to my mind. I felt Chetna was going through exactly what I had undergone. Nothing more appropriate or better could come out of me at this stage. I turned the Punjabi into the Hindi version and re-lived with Chetna what I had gone through fifteen years earlier:

> *Today we took the cloud-lip*
> *From the bowl of the sky*
> *And supped—a sip of moonlight.*

Nina in *Aalna* was conceived totally in my imagination. In the course of my writing it, Nina's personality so took hold of me that I dreamt about her one night. She was standing beside me, full of rage and breathing hard, and she said: 'Why did you have to end my life so painfully? Just tell me why . . . Why? What would you have lost by letting me live? I wanted life. Why did you have to take it away . . .? Why?'

At a point in the novella, Nina reflects sadly: 'My mother did not find any happiness in life. Perhaps she was me in a previous existence. And now, in the next life that I've been given, I have been denied happiness again. Will I find happiness when I am reincarnated in the life of my daughter?'

Aalna was not influenced by any belief in the doctrine of the transmigration of souls. What I was trying to do was to find a nexus in the saga of three generations. The story so took hold of one of my readers that she identified herself wholly with Nina. She was possessed by the thought that she would have to die and be reborn to attain the happiness that had eluded her in this life. She sent a series of letters to me—without disclosing her identity. All she kept saying was, 'I am the Nina of your book!' I wanted to pull her out of that illusion. But I had no way of communicating with her. Alas! I never found out what became of her.

When *Ik si Anita* was published in Urdu, a prostitute by descent from Hyderabad, wrote to say that the story was of her life. Her soul was as pure, her search as similar. The difference lay only in the sequence of events. She gave me details about herself with the offer to come in person to Delhi, should I want to know anything more about her. I extended her an invitation but for whatever good reasons she had, she chose to change her mind. Perhaps someone compelled her to do it. Anyhow, I do not know what became of her either.

The heroine of *Aerial* came and lived with me for a full month and a half before I could get her out of my system. She was the first person to hear the novella when it was completed. During the reading she often wept tears of satisfaction of a sort. This satisfaction is of greater value to me than the fact of publication. I am convinced a work of art is primarily meant for study. It is never intended to be the cause of pain to anybody . . . nor, for that matter, to motivate such abominable rumours as seem to be the obsession of some Punjabi writers.

Bulava was based on Faiz, the distinguished painter from Bombay, who not only squandered away whatever money came to his hands, but his life too, on horse races. Both his art, and the death wish, came from the same passion moving in paradoxically opposite directions. I made a desperate attempt to arrest his wasted years in this novella. And, in conformity with my normal practice, had him read it before sending it to the press.

One of my stories is of the charming, self-effacing wife of a diplomat. I had it translated into English for her to see before I sought her permission for its publication. I wrote two stories on the most critical and painful years of a dear friend of mine. At her instance, however, I changed the names of cities and characters in such a way that not even her closest relatives could find any point of contact.

The ending of the story on a foreign woman had to be changed. She dies in my story. But when I fell into her warm embrace on my visit to her country, her first words were, 'See, I'm still alive and kicking!' We went and had photographs taken of us together and she bought me many souvenirs!

My wealth really and truly consists in the characters I have created and in the love that binds me to them. I have never understood what those who cause pain to anyone achieve in their writings.

Tanvir in *Jebkatre* writes a poem from jail, which he manages to send out for publication under the signature *Prisoner No. 68/9*. This particular number came to my mind unthinkingly at the time of writing. Later, it struck me that Gorky had borne it when he was in jail. I had noted it in my diary when I had gone to see the house in Moscow where he had once lived.

It is odd how the streams of the conscious and subconscious keep merging and diverting their courses.

Jebkatre was based on the relatively immature years of my son's life. I had written a story earlier under the title *Kahani dar Kahani* that told of the incident of my son's letter to a Bengali girlfriend during the vacations. A Beethoven record was being played at the time, the Fifth Symphony. To the strain of the opening bars he wrote: 'Writing to you is like knocking at one's own door.' The reply was straight and simple. In the deepening darkness of the evening twilight when he came with it in his hand, I knew nothing at all about their correspondence. 'Mamma! She hasn't understood what I wrote—shall I read it out to you?' He read out from the rough copy he had retained of it. 'The reply is like talking about the weather.' 'Will you be wanting to write to her again?' 'Certainly not! It's like entering a house at the front door and coming from the back one.' This prompted me to write the story. The novella that was to follow needed a much vaster canvas. The atmosphere of University hostel life around my son's circle . . . as they grow, they are astonished at their own dreams; they flirt with hunger, time and fear; they view life from their own angles; and they live with the pains and joys of their own experience.

My son and his friends go through the usual joys and pains of growth. Mine was really an undertaking to understand the next generation. I saw myself as a spectator, looking into their thoughts from outside. After completing *Jebkatre,* I gave it to my son to read. It is just possible some of his friends read it sooner than he could and they recognized themselves, each one of them, and praised handsomely what I had been able to achieve. When it came to my son, he put in the margin in some places the word 'super'. Still, he was not entirely satisfied. 'Had I written it, it would have been altogether different,' he said. My total endeavour was to bridge the generation gap. In building this bridge, the pace had to be my own . . . generation removed.

Long after the novella had been published, Savita and Ravi, whose marriage is described in it at some length, came to see my son and also met me. They were highly amused to read about themselves while I was as intrigued seeing characters from my books stepping out to confront me . . .

Coming back to the creative processes, when first the idea of *Jebkatre* came to my mind, I had just received from my son, a letter, with which the fifth chapter of my book begins. Kapil, the hero, writes the letter in the form of a news bulletin, *The Times of Kapil.* He gives the date of inception and of publication. That incidentally is the date of his own birthday; he plans six columns—each for a different item—and thus ingeniously weaves the newsletter for the benefit of his mother . . .

My son's name is Navraj. But the nickname 'Sally' by which we usually call him, is endearingly stamped on the letter, *The Times of Sally.* I still have the letter.

Whenever he came home for the vacation, Navraj used to be full of all sorts of hostel news. From his model newsletter I made such notes as I needed before I really sat down to write the story. I was in the midst of it when he startled me one day with his sudden intrusion: 'It was all very well for you, Mamma, to give a new turn to your life . . . but did you ever stop to think what mental suffering we two children of yours went through?'

When a house crumbles I know how much of the dust raised rubs into the sensitive skins of children and causes them pain.

I know, alas, only too well what they had gone through . . . My daughter all along was full of sympathy for me, but my son for a time was affected by what others said . . . he was then in his teens. The inherent difference between their attitudes of course lay in the fact that one was a boy and the other a girl, although she too was at the time still in her formative years. Whenever Navraj was pensive and crotchety, she consoled me with words which echo in my ears even today. 'Don't you worry, Mamma, he'll understand when he is older.'

To continue, Sally challenged me one day: 'Mamma! Can you project the suffering of a child when a home breaks down?'

'Why not?' And I did indeed depict as well as I could the state of his mind in *Midnight Fears* . . .

But only those have given me pain who have had nothing whatsoever to do with me in life. Their rancour was because I happened to be a contemporary creative artist. I have not suffered at the hands of my readers nor at the hands of those who have shared what I have had to bear.

The friendship between Basu Bhattacharya and Imroz and I has flourished. Basu has been worn down by his life of poverty but he never lets anyone know about it. He has rebelled against the great director and producer in the film world, Bimal Roy, who declined to him the hand of Rinki, his daughter. Not one to be discouraged, Basu whisked his 'Ideal of Beauty' away, sat her by his side, and shut poverty firmly out. 'As lord and master of my own home it will not cross the threshold . . . without my permission! How could it dare to?' I too think that whatever I am churning out of my mind is really for those who steadfastly change conventional norms, and form new patterns of life with truth alone as their beacon-light.

The Magic of Imaginative Invention

There was a time in my life when I let my imagination run away with me . . .

I had heard the word 'magic' in the stories they told me in my childhood, but experienced it only on the day it came masked as my alter ego and then stretched itself out on the sap of my life . . . This was about the time my son became the prop of my hopes, towards the end of 1946.

I had read about how a child develops and how his mind is shaped by his mother's thoughts . . . My imagination drew me away from the world around me and I said to myself: If you always have Sahir's face in your mind's eye, he'll grow to resemble him.

I know that I was merely feeding my frustrations . . .

Like divinity aiming at the creation of a wonderful one . . .
Free from the claims of the flesh . . .
Free from all that flesh and blood has been heir to
From the dawn of creation . . .

In this state of crazy love, when my baby was born on July 3, 1947, and I first looked upon his face, it was the face of Sahir in my mind . . .

Alas! one cannot live forever in an imagined world and I grew out of this state by talking in terms of a fairy tale . . .

Laughing at myself, I related the entire episode once to Sahir. I do not know what exactly his reaction was. I only know that he laughed it all away with the casual remark: 'Very poor taste!'

Once he took my daughter in his lap and said: 'Shall I tell you a story?' And when she was all attention, he began, 'There was once a woodcutter who chopped the wood of the forest by night and by day. Then one day he caught sight of a lovely princess and he wanted to run away with her . . .'

'And then?' She was at an age when a child can be very attentive and very curious.

I did not interrupt and also began to listen . . . 'And the woodcutter stood at a distance, gazing with eyes of wonder at the princess and then he sadly got back to hacking and chopping the wood. Now don't you think it is a true story?'

'Of course it is . . . I saw it all with my own eyes!' Why she said that on the spur of the moment I cannot say.

Sahir gave me a meaningful look, 'See, she knows it all.' He cajoled her. 'You were there in the wood, weren't you?'

She nodded her head.

And he prodded her with the next question: 'You saw the woodcutter as well, did you? Who was he?'

For a split second she hesitated, and then she blurted out 'You!' 'And who was the princess?'

'Mamma!' She chuckled.

'See how much they know! See how observant children can be!' Sahir said.

Years went by. In 1960, when I was in Bombay, I was drawn close to Rajinder Singh Bedi. We often met. Later one evening, he took me off guard by asking, 'I heard Prakash Pandit say that Sahir was Navraj's father?'

So I told him the entire story of my madness. 'Correct, imaginatively; incorrect, factually.'

Navraj was about thirteen when he too said, 'Mamma! Can I ask you a question? Will you tell me the truth?'

'Certainly!'

'Am I Uncle Sahir's son?'

'No . . .'

'If I am . . . do tell me . . . I like him.'

'So do I, son! But if what you think was the real truth, I would really and truly have told you.'

My son was convinced of the truth.

But I wondered if imaginative truth was in any way less powerful . . .

Whenever Sahir came to see me in Lahore, it was as if he had somehow been conjured up by my silences. He had become so much a part of them, sitting still in the chair until it was time for him to go away . . .

He would quietly go on chain-smoking . . . he would smoke half a cigarette, stub it out, and light another. When he was gone, the place was littered with cigarette ends . . .

Sometimes, I intensely longed to touch him but I could not overcome my own reservations.

It was a time when I lived in my imagination a great deal.

When he was gone, I would collect the stubs and preserve them secretly in a little cupboard. And then I would salvage them one by one and quietly sit and light them, one after the other . . . and I would feel the touch of his fingers by holding the stubs he once had held . . .!

That was how I got into the habit of smoking. I used to feel his presence from the aroma around . . . And from the smoke curling up I would see his form emerging like a genie . . .

It was this experience that found expression in my novella *Iksi Anita* . . . although I do not think Sahir has any knowledge of all this.

The world of the imagination belongs only to those who create it. Yet the figures of the imagination take on a power all their own.

When in the dawn of creation the earth was a blazing mass of fire millions of years ago, and man came into being, he had neither fear nor pleasure in solitude.

On the splitting up of his body, when one half became man and the other woman . . . the creation of mankind began . . .

But the history of creation must not be interpreted to mean merely a history of the past. Each period of time has its own history . . . Each of the littlest of the little peoples of the world have their own history . . .

I too . . .

Truth and the Author

I had several times met Dhuswan Swamy, the Cultural Secretary at the Nepalese Embassy in New Delhi. He was a greater writer than the diplomat he was by rank and calling. He became a close friend and shared with me whatever problem of the moment weighed him down. The story *Adalat* was about him and his own particular condition. I decided to include it in an anthology I was compiling in Hindi, *Punjab ton Baharlay Pattar.* When the book was in press, I passed on the information to him. The name of the country to which the character belonged was to be printed at the end of the story. But envisaging the possibility of trouble for him if he allowed that fact to be divulged, he sought the deletion of the reference to his country. Not wanting him to suffer in any way, I put down 'Assam' instead of 'Nepal'. The book was at last published and he went through it. He promptly sat down and wrote a note permitting me to include at the relevant place, whenever I chose to write my autobiography, the following note:

> This story is based on Dhuswan—but the respected Cultural Counsellor is so faint of heart that in the earlier publication his country of origin was concealed.

In my eyes, he went up greatly in esteem. . . as a writer, he could not but be honest.

This story had such a deep effect on him that he read it out to his wife, as well as to his girlfriend. Then he had a rather disturbing dream. He put it on paper and sent it to me:

I do not know whether it was the hour of dawn or evening . . . dusky twilight had spread across the sky. I was being swept down by the gravitational pull of a rushing stream. I used to cross it every day but on this particular occasion I faltered for fear that I should lose my footing on seeing the woman (now married, with two children) I loved. I walked along the bank until I saw two tents pitched in the stretching sands. Craning my neck to peer inside I saw a man I could recognize well: whose thoughts and feelings too I could see through as clearly as clearly can be. In front of him stood three young girls, each dressed differently, but exactly alike in appearance. The man was struck dumb because one of the three was his beloved. What test was this illusion subjecting him to? Seeing him in this state, one of them winced a little and then flung herself into his arms. Immediately a man from the next tent came out and erupted with words hotter than molten lava, 'What's wrong with you? What can you do with him? He's married! He is worse than a bee that flits from flower to flower.' The girl drew back. 'What are you telling me? Don't I know? I'll make sure that he's mine pretty soon . . .' And what did I see next? The man's head floated off out of sight into space! The first man then swept the girl off her feet with an impassioned embrace. And I thought to myself that both the headless one and the other were being dissolved into me. With that shock I woke up and saw Amrita Pritam's anthology open by my side at the page of the story *Ik Shahr di Maut* that I had been reading when I had fallen asleep.

I become so involved with the characters of my creation that their sufferings become my own. A relationship is established with all of them. But someone like Dhuswan wins not only my love and sympathy, but also a place of respect for himself.

Pitch-black Clouds

There is a poem I wrote at about this time:

> *Such a holocaust there was today–*
> *All books and magazines from my shelves*
> *. . . ripped off each other's*
> *Covers, shredded each other's page in their rage*
> *So that the mirrors of my thoughts cracked and fell.*
> *All the world's races and creeds*
> *Stifled and throttled each other . . .*
> *With their twisted, interlocked limbs . . .*
> *Maps of countries, demarcated frontiers*
> *Fell prey to cataclysmic war.*
> *But what left me thunderstruck was*
> *The deep black poison (So rich red*
> *From the blood that was shed!)*
> *Of some of the books and the papers*
> *Involved in the explosion . . .*

Sadness had been growing steadily for some time and on that day it began hovering threateningly like dark clouds. Journalism of low level; rumours spread by contemporaries; these had cast menacing shadows over religious sects, social organizations and political cells with their deep black corrosive poison . . .

Perhaps that was the reason why, with such deep pain I place the written word above everything else. When the Chinese invaded Samarkand in 751 AD and were defeated by the Arabs, and when the latter learnt the art of making paper from them, the first poem on the first sheet was written . . . the thrill of the hand that wrote it passes into mine! O Lord . . .

A Salute

On August 18, 1973, I had a call from Ashoka Hotel. 'I'm a member of the Pakistani Peace Delegation . . .'

I had barely begun lunch. I did not finish it. I checked what the time was. In another half an hour, the man who had called me on the telephone arrived to deliver a letter and a book from Sajjad . . .

He arrived on the dot! He read the verse by Faiz inscribed on the lamp-shade and Kazmi on the door of the library and I began the conversation. 'You must square things up this time. Consider, after all, what enmity can there be with a country when lines from her poets come out alive on these walls.'

He replied promptly: 'There will be peace, God willing!'

When the good messenger had departed, I opened the letter. A magic spell was instantly cast over me. 'I cannot let go any opportunity of writing to you . . . Whenever any noble soul crosses the frontier, I take it. I had my letter to you posted from Rome by one of the men who accompanied the first President of our country on his visit there. I trust you got it. I trust you will

receive this one too. The messenger is a good friend of mine
. . . He'll be getting the opportunity to meet you . . . I've been
badly wanting to see you, so badly . . . even if I can through the
eyes of a friend I'll consider myself happy. I've asked him to
ring you up and find out if such a meeting is possible. Should
it materialize, on his return I'll pester him for days on end with
question after question: What did she look like? How was she
dressed? Did she smile? What did she have to say about me? Is
she still the same? And a hundred questions more. He is lucky
. . . I am thirsty for a fleeting moment . . .

Khalil Gibran wrote: 'The aim of life is to reach out to its
secrets. Madness is the only way . . .' I thought Sajjad was my
Khalil Gibran then. I pride in my madness, but even that has
bowed in salute to Sajjad!

God-like Support

There have been so many days when I have held my pen close
to my breast and wept and wept.

It is impossible to say who comes to support you like a
god and when.

My pen has always been the perceptible; I can see it with
my eyes. It has always been the tangible, I can touch it with my
hands and like a blank sheet of paper, I can hold it to my heart.

During the past half century, I have had passing fancies
for many things. First, it was photography. Father had a dark
room in the house. That was how I started developing film, and

from the negative, marvelled at the process that turned it into a positive, clear, glistening picture, emerged from nothingness. I was for some time at it, until dancing became an absorbing passion with me. For six to eight months I received lessons from no less a person than Tara Chowdhry at Lahore. But when she invited me to perform with her, permission to go on the stage was flatly refused. Some desires withered like dried leaves; others went to seed. Then came the time for them to sprout again with new vigour. This time, it was the sitar. Master Ram Rakha, Siraj Ahmed and Dina Sitariya were my *gurus*. My fondness for tennis came next. I went for daily lessons to the Lawrence Garden courts. All these hobbies died, with Partition.

Life offered neither the leisure nor the facilities any more. Facing me was the grim problem of existence. By sheer chance I met M S Randhawa, who wrote to the Station Director of All India Radio, and got me a job. I stuck to it for a full twelve years . . . the first few of which were on a daily contract of ₹5! I could not therefore afford to lie on a sick bed even for a day! It was agony, to go on working when I had a cold or a fever. I am reminded of a colleague from my section, Kumar, who took upon himself to help me out by doing the longer announcements himself, and leaving the shorter ones to me.

The one thing that did not let me down during the most depressing times was my pen. Whether I wrote my own thoughts down, or wrote about Partition, my pen was as much a part of me as the limbs of my body. The pen was the decisive factor in my life. Other interests only served as manure to germinate the seeds that bore fruit in due course.

What is it that nourishes the appetite one has for certain things of life? The friendships with Sahir and Sajjad blossom at the same time as my relationship with Imroz . . . and they turn life into a veritable oasis.

A couple of years ago I met Sahir. The pressure he put on me was so great that I could not but go and stay with him for two days. On my return to Delhi, I wrote:

Strange meeting—after many years
When two lives throbbed like a poem . . .

But despite the ecstasy of such throbs, I perceived the plight Imroz was in. As he put it, 'I plead guilty for the year 1960 . . . But my guilt lay in the green years of my youth.' And though I wrote poems like *Janam Jali* on his professed 'guilt', I could still say with composure: 'And are our guilts heinous offences?'

I speak of today. I cannot say how many yesterdays have nourished this today.

I could will this 'today' to be with me all my life but no matter how unwillingly it turned into a tomorrow too, I would say: 'Our offences are not heinous.'

Imroz is six years my junior. I cannot bear rough weather any more while he can brave all climates. So I often smile and say: 'God grants the too-brief period of youth to one and all; to me He has in His greatness, granted two! Mine petered off; Imroz's came on! Now that I have two 'todays', what fear then can I have of tomorrow?

Years ago, I wrote:

I eat what I earn—
Not yesterday's left-overs—
And leave no grain for tomorrow

My 'today' left me scarred. I accepted that. And now it has brought in serenity. Should I have to part with anything, should I have to depart any moment now, I would be able to do so with serenity. My only wish is that those who have had nothing to do with me in life, should have nothing to do with me after my death . . . This I say because there are people who have nothing in common with one but who will form part of the crowds gathering around one at such a time. I never had much to do with rites and rituals. They should not take the trouble of taking part in true or false funeral orations and condolence meetings and rallies . . .

There was hardly a Punjabi paper or magazine I could be sure of not printing some calumny against me (So often, even before I had the chance to go through them, Imroz would cut the bits that contained adverse comments. I wrote about this in *Dilli diyan Gallian.* Imroz, incidentally, is Nasir in that book.) To the extent he could, Imroz shielded me from such suffering. I can therefore depend on him not to allow any untruths to get anywhere near my dead body.

My children and he, between them, know how to deal with my remains . . . they must have the honour.

The practice at one time was for people to place jars full of water and vessels of silver and gold by the side of a body. I have no faith in any such thing. Not that one has to have faith in everything, but I would like Imroz to let my pen go with me.

Man is, in Eric Hoffter's word, 'an incomplete creation of God'. He struggles and endeavours therefore to complete what He has left unfinished. An observation I once made in my novella *Yatri,* is relevant. 'The effort is to reach the beyond to the best of my ability.' Reading Eric Hoffter I have felt that the struggle and endeavour to reach the beyond entailed the task of 'completion' in that sense. That is why my last wish is that the pen that stood by me all the way through should be with me even after my journey has come to end.

Greater Truths . . . and Smaller

With loving care I water the plants I have around the house. While I am at this daily exercise, Imroz keeps shuffling up and down with me reading out the news from the paper in his hands. Admiring the money-plant's rapid growth I drew his attention to it one morning. 'See how it grows, like a creeper.' As wittily as ever he remarked: 'By your showers, you could make Waris Shah put out tendrils and shoots. This is after all a plant . . .'

Sometimes, pain and joy appear to be two sides of the same coin. So I said, 'The Waris Shah plant is watered both from my love and tears. But do you remember the time of my first meeting with you?' My name was proposed for the chairmanship of a certain conference in Jullundur and a leader of the Communist Party raised a strong voice of protest. 'No . . . we will not allow her sullied name to have anything to do with

us! We will be ruined . . .' That very evening, Khalsa College in
Delhi arranged a reception in my honour. That of course came
after my University honours. That protest of the Communist
leader was still deeply engraved in my mind when in my speech
of thanks I said: 'Be it through a moment of anonymity, glory,
or infamy . . . a writer will always remain a writer . . .!'

With the passage of time I have been able to define the
seasons of life as those of anonymity, glory and infamy. I have
passed through all, though it was all a long time ago. The longest
and the most grim was the first.

With Imroz, it has certainly not been roses, roses, all the
way. Our association has had its troughs and its heights . . . two
beings oscillating between merging and clashing . . . merging
like the water of streams and clashing like rival peaks. After
fourteen years' experience (which was exactly the period of
Lord Rama's exile) I have no regrets about the path chosen
by us.

Imroz's personality is like the flow of a river, uncontrolled
by locks and sluices. Should he be restrained, Imroz would
impetuously divert his course. A relationship with him can last
only so long as there is nothing to bind it. Unfortunately, in life
there is not much natural freedom. There is society and there
is the law. His view is: 'Why should the law interfere when
you choose a path for yourself alone. To subject such choice to
restraint of any kind is an insult both to the feet and to the path.'

The effect his first meeting had on me, had a lot to do with
the high fever I was in at the time. That evening he touched

my forehead for the first time, 'Is it very bad?' After this he said the words, 'In this one day, I've put the weight of years on my back.' And becoming aware of the emptiness in our lives, he went on. 'There can be no one else . . . no one . . . you are my daughter . . . I, your son.' And although the reasons for the degrading of his friendship are unfounded, its effect is not.

Imroz goes into rages of fury, and I am sad. Then for hours we are submerged in our silences, silences very deep. But until the truth descends, need it be asked why a cushion in the drawing room lies upside down or why there is an empty packet of cigarettes on the *divan?* Why was the bottle of glue not put back in its place or the garage shutter not pulled down after the car was in? Time comes to a stop. Silence alone reigns supreme. The only sound that ends this silence is of the door as it shuts when he has gone into his room.

Hours pass in this way, as if time was gasping for breath! Then the silence gives way to the beauty of the words Imroz breaks it with: 'Here we are! Giving each other the yogic exercises necessary for our health!'

That is why I refer to all such troughs as the smaller truths, and his existence as the great one. The Hindi poet, Kailash Vajpeyi, once observed, 'The Moon was in the House of Fate when you were born.' Humorously, I parried, 'He must have left it after waiting for two and a half hours . . .' Imroz cut in, 'Imroz could not have budged once he had entered; the Moon is of a different mould altogether. Flitting from house to house is his habit, is it not?'

I am reminded of what I said to him once when I was ill. 'Promise me that when I am gone, you will not live alone. There is plenty of beauty and youth around in the world.'

He replied with some passion: 'Who, by the way, do you take me for? A Parsee . . . that I must be thrown to the vultures to be pecked at . . .? You've no business to die on my hands like this . . . when I haven't yet had one desire of mine fulfilled? I must see the film through. Now you promise me you're going to jog along until we're both ready to go together . . .'

Those words gave to the truth of the moment an extra dimension. My suffering is the lesser truth when weighted against the greater truth of the happiness of life with him . . .

Life with him is like the fragrance of flowers, which does not fade with wear. I once said to him, 'So few seem to be the days left to me now that I have decided to enjoy myself as if I were at great God's own wedding day!' He took a moment to understand the point of my remark, and then remarked, 'Am I not to be at the feast?' I was not to be outwitted. 'True . . . true . . . but you're from the bride's side . . . I'm of the groom's party!' So, from that day the joke stretched on and on and Imroz would say: 'Not to worry . . . leave this to us . . . We're from the bride's side, aren't we? Aren't we to be at the service of the groom's party?'

I have seen the bickerings that go on at weddings, but in my friendship with Imroz, I've had the rare feeling of being the good God's true wedding guest!

For years, I have not been able to do without a cook. I had become so dependent that whenever the cook was indisposed, I felt utterly lost! But for the last seventeen years, I have not had any. I got into the habit of cooking with my own hands from the time we were with Sobha Singhji, the famous Punjabi artist, at Andretta. Imroz and I were most uncomfortable when his old wife was put to such great bother on our account. The first time I tried lending a hand, I could not even raise a log fire. Imroz undertook to do it and I decided I would do the cooking. We got used to doing things on our own. On our return we felt the servant was somehow always in the way! And so for the last seventeen years or so, we have done without one. Of course, we have part time arrangements, with a boy for the washing and cleaning up. For the rest, we are self-sufficient. Should it happen that the part time help is taken ill or is on leave, well then, we divide the work between us. If I scrub the dishes, Imroz helps by heating and pouring the water for the washing and so on. But should he happen to be absorbed in his studio work, I finish up and then call out: 'Hey, you from the bride's side, any progress today? The groom's party has done the rubbing and the scrubbing.' And so, the joke stretches on.

Imroz's is an expensive art. The canvasses, the brushes and the paints are costly things. And when he runs out of funds, I say to him: 'I've bought your last picture. Here's the money. Now run along and buy yourself a new canvas . . .' When the sales proceeds of my books are delayed and I am dismayed, he does likewise: 'Come on! I buy over the rights to such-and-such story for my screenplay! Here's the advance on it . . .!' Who bothers whether the money changes hands or not, we play the make-believe game and, what is of the greatest value, keep up our morale by such stratagems. The hardest of times seem easy enough to go through. I keep buying odd things out of sight in nooks and corners of cupboards and trunks for a birthday or souvenir. I have always managed to dig out something to serve as a gift when there is no time to sniff around in shops. From some bank pass-book or the other, I can check the price of the article as well. In the same way, I can always salvage something or the other from the refrigerator when anyone is hungry between meals. Imroz is quite tickled by this habit of mine. He laughs: 'You must have shoved in something of me somewhere for your future life, I bet!'

Considering everything, I must surely have saved something in my previous birth for this one . . . when I have been able to drink my fill even when desert sands stretched far out to the distant horizon . . . I wish what he said in jest turns out to be true so I do save something of him for my next life as well.

A Poem Explained

On the night of September 5, 1973, at around 10.30, while I was reading Kazantzakis' *Rock Garden,* the Vice-Chancellor of a certain University rang up: 'At the next senate meeting a resolution is to be passed. Your story *Ik Shahr di Maut* is to be banned. I knew your father and looked up to him in esteem. So I thought it only proper that I should let you know. Your story is about the death of a city. I do hope this does not mean your death as a writer . . .'

I heard the news calmly. The Vice-Chancellor was really sorry for me. I thanked him for his kind sympathy and courtesy and casually asked, 'But have you read the story?'

'No. I do not profess to know much about literature. My field is science.'

'True. But, I trust your wisdom. Would you kindly go through it once?'

'I have the synopsis here. That's not too flattering, I'm afraid. . .'

'A synopsis can be misleading.'

'How can that be?'

'Why not? If one writes with a prejudiced mind.'

'Maybe . . . yet . . .'

'When the original piece is available, it is not much trouble going through it . . .'

'Should an official of this University, perhaps the Registrar himself, call on you, would you kindly discuss the thing with him?'

'If you will read it yourself and then give me a ring. I'd much rather discuss with you . . .'

'Well now, let me see. Shall we make it sometime next week? Sorry to have disturbed you at this late hour, but I have the same regard for you as I had for your father and his lofty outlook.'

'How can you judge me? Without reading me, I mean . . .'

'Then why don't you write in a way we'd be compelled to respect you?'

'Don't you worry. As long as my conscience is clear.'

Like my name, my honour has not depended on others. When the call was over, Imroz's face lit up with a smile as mine did. He had been listening in and now laughed outright. He said: 'I thought resolutions of bodies like University senates are for positive purposes. Aren't they disgracing themselves by using them for such cheap ends?'

At about this time, Suresh Kohli was at work translating *Ik Shahr di Maut* for inclusion in an anthology covering almost all the regional languages of the country. Bharatiya Jnanpith was due to release a book of my selected works in which, incidentally, this story was also to figure. The story was given pride of place in *Punjab ton Bharlay Pattar* which was being brought out by Rajpal Press. And yet this was the story that would be condemned at a University senate meeting! Even if it had not been acclaimed at diverse levels, I knew in my heart of hearts that it reflected the best of my writing. I had great satisfaction writing it and I know that a whole volume of University resolutions would not harm it.

But I was sad. The whole episode rekindled unhappy memories. From the day I started to write, these voices of derision have always been with me. Perhaps they will always be there for ever and ever.

As was his practice, Davinder Satyarthi Sahib had then launched another one of his scurrilous attacks on me in some paper. He was never close enough to claim to know me. Yet he always wrote as though he suffered personal anguish on my account. It was perhaps this article which was responsible for my melancholic mood at the time. As a matter of fact there was more to it. It was not just one article but a continuing strain of viciousness. Sick of it all, I sat down and wrote the poem *Farewell*.

A poet does not have to give a detailed analysis of his work. But this poem was different. It was indirect in its allusions. At first reading, it could well give the impression of being the story of some personal tragedy but the epicycle is really woven around Punjab. And this province is to me like the face of a beloved surrounded by a vacuous crowd of self-seeking strangers. It went:

O Lord! The immobility is
Thine own hymn on Thyself
I have neither rhythm
Nor poetic diction to
Meet Thee in rhyme
Emanating from Thee
All too silently . . .
As meanings flow from words.
And, speaking of meanings unfortunate—
All depends really on their flow:
If say . . . life today finds some meaning
Some idiotic twist could be given to it tomorrow!
But a poem survives such contentiousnesses . . .

Therefore, O Lord—let Thy longevity be
Coextensive with Thine own hymn on Thee!

I am proud of my existence. If the earth of Punjab is like a poem, I am the meaning of the poem. Meanings have to be sought out. Those of today may not be acceptable tomorrow. I seek nothing more than such limited understanding as exists . . . So long as this poem that is Punjab, survives, all is well. Because I seek silently to pass from the scene, I have written what I have and say my *Farewell*.

5

THE PHOENIX DYNASTY

History tells us of the Phoenicians who got their name from the phoenix with which they identified themselves. The phoenix rises again and again from its own ashes. Those human races which arose with renewed vigour from near destruction, in that act of rising also seem to give strength to the dead and the dying. There lies the glory of the phoenix legend.

The phoenix is also associated with the cult of sun worship, the sun that rises and sets. This is no more symbolic association. No historian can tell precisely where the Phoenicians came from. The conjecture is that they could have been from any region from the middle of Egypt to India. Anyhow the practice of sun worship is widespread. One of the names they gave to the sun was *Un,* and *Allendane* in England was one of the places they settled in during their wandering in search of a place they could call their own.

When the twelve tribes of Israel fanned out through the centuries to different parts of the world there was some integration with Phoenician blood. Thus the root of the word 'England' is traceable to Hebrew. The bull was the symbol of Joseph and his brethren. The Hebrew word for 'bull' is 'angle'. The new land these people found thus became 'Angland'.

My only justification for this diversion into historical complexities is that we in Punjab also seem to bear some kind of relationship with the Phoenicians. In Punjabi we refer to the Phoenicians as *Kuknoosi*. The best writers in the world, I think, are *Kuknoosi,* that is to say, they consume themselves in the fire of creation and rise again from the ashes to take on new images.

A long time ago I wrote *Sooraj te Syal,* a self-analytical article in which some part of me seemed to go down with the setting sun. And as the sun rose, some other part reached out to the high heavens. The night is a murky abysmal tunnel for me that ends when the sun comes up. I said in *Sooraj te Syal:* 'All this did not happen consciously. How did it happen then? Who knows? I have only tried to rationalize.' I remember when I was very young I would start crying as the sun set and it grew dark. Mother would comfort me. She would say: 'Now shut your eyes and the sun will come!' Yet every night I would ask the same question: 'But why does it have to go away everyday?'

The symbol of the sun kept recurring in my poems for a good many years. In the year 1973 for example, when I took a cursory look at my work in chronological order, a positive pattern seemed to emerge.

The first and the most forceful reference to the sun was in the partition year, 1947 that is, when an unwanted child of a raped and abducted woman laments:

> *That contempt am I; bearing the fate of the befallen . . .*
> *On descent into the world when star after star has fallen . . .*
> *When the light of the sun has been snuffed out . . .*

Then come the dreams linked up with realities of independence in *Main Tavarikhhan Hindi di . . .* and the choral refrain,

> *The moon rising in the sky bows down to this day*
> *The sun too offers salutations . . . the same way.*

The sun image was again dominant in the intensity of my personal passion in 1953.

> *The rays dipped into the sun and crimson hues spread*
> *On the earth that lay silvery-white under the moon's*
> *rays . . . We dipped the earth*
> *In the sun we'd dissolved . . .*

> *The East sifted the layers of the skies*
> *With the bowl of the sun in hand*
> *And dyed them saffron . . .*

> *The sun made some henna-paste*
> *And graciously dyed the palms as though*
> *It was dying our fate.*

I was seeing for the first time the image of the sun as a bowl of milk laced with saffron, and the comparison of its red colour with henna. A note of sadness pervades the rest of the poem:

The sun capsizes with the western billows
And the evening shadows close in on us . . .

I set fire to the suns and lit up the moons of my life . . .
I sought the stars from the skies to stud the silver,
But none came forth to light the torch . . .
So life got swamped by deep black darknesses
Till they were sifted and scattered by the fire of life's
long years . . .

The eastern horizon melted away
The heavy skies with intense light . . .
The rising sun flailed and threshed the night
And whipped off the murky miles . . .
And his bright rays shone again . . .

The sun lay scorched, with his rays straw-like . . .
Fanned by zephyrs the East lit up her fires,
The rays sparked up into leaping-dancing flames . . .
And out come the fields fringed around with seats . . .
Come along, Stranger-traveller! Who knows what
the morrow brings?

The sun turned his back
And December ties up its sticks . . .
Fled again are the 365 days that once existed!
I congratulate myself on my own fire . . .
The sun came to my door
And took a live coal from me to light his . . .

The rays pierce into
The delicate parts of the heart
And set flame the dormant longings

I try to fly
Yet I do not succeed.
And a fringe of my veil catches fire

The suns and moons are squaring up accounts . . .
Both the scales fill to spilling over their share of light . . .

Life! Do not shut on me your door . . .
My task is not yet over . . .
The sun is scattering his light
and the earth its odour!

The smell of dreams is still on the lips of sleep,
The first ray set its auspicious mark on the forehead
of night . . .
And I weave my sacred veil with threads of longings
all my own
And through the death-rattle of parting comes the lilting
wedding note of the shehnai

Whoever heated the oven of night . . . ?
See how its lid is being taken off by the sun!

Ye who own the earth
Hear all this
As Guru Arjun Dev's through his ordeal
Love again has been put in a boiling cauldron . . .

The tree of the sun is still there, shining.
But someone has broken the rays—the branches,
And the sky is hung with the moon-lace
That someone has torn off.

The sun-horse neighed
The saddle of light fell,
Walking on for ages . . .
The traveller wept.

The sun is a skiff, it sinks with the coming western waves; it is a ball of cotton, flailed by a simoon; it is a bamboo forest that dries up and is scorched; it is nothing without the tumultuous passion of the heart, seeking to light its fire from a live coal borrowed from me; it is so many needles put together that prick and are gone through my delicate fingers; it is a boiling cauldron in which my love is tried; it is a tree from which someone has broken off its branching rays; it is a horse from which the saddle of light has fallen away, so many are the aspects of the sun that I see.

Unresolved, through nightlong darkness I sit
My scar will not let me sleep
With sunlight overhead
Where can I hide the scar?

A conscious effort thus is sometimes discernible. Again:

It's dawn now
Like a shaft a sun-ray darts through my heart . . .

Passing through the various houses, life ends where it began, that is, with the sun. I was not fully aware of the process when I described those nuances. Although now when I try to analyse myself:

The current that swept through the floodgates of my heart
Carried a voice: that my footfalls would be heard in other lands,
The rays beckoned me forth:
Arise now! And travel to the House of the Sun . . .

Apart from the love poems, the sun image has penetrated many others. As for instance this one, of my meeting with Ho Chi Minh:

Today even the winds
Asked of Vietnam,
Who wiped a tear
From the cheek of history?
In the early hours of the morning
The earth dreamed a verdant dream;
Who rose to the fields of heaven
And sowed the sun?

And I wrote of the earth emaciated from the horrors of war:

Earth sent a messenger to find out
Who would write the lullabies of the future?
They say: hope lies in the womb of a ray

The East is setting up its cradle—
Its eternal cradle.
Night is pregnant with the tun.

Earth, as midwife, prays:
May night never be barren!
And pain, never sterile!

All these poems were written between 1947 and 1959. In the thirteen years that follow, the motif of the sun keeps on being repeated:

I recall the time
When a patch of sunshine
Held the sun's finger

While seeing the darkness fair
Yet, got lost in the throngs!

You are like the sun.
Let me lift a corner of my rug
And warm my hands and feet . . .
I will drink in a breath
My fill of the sun . . .
Then let a drop of it
Fall in my womb . . .
I give birth to a sun every day
And every day
It is orphaned.

Lines on personalities like Lenin and Guru Nanak also contain reference to the sun:

You meet me like a new day
Like changed dates again and again,
Emerging from my wall calendar:
Strange character of my history
From the calendar to the streets
You walk: a sunlight blazes . . .

The cravings of unripe pregnancy:
The restless heart.
I sit to churn and the butter flows.
In the pitcher I put my hands
And see a sweet sunball on my palm . . .

The monologue by Sulakhni, Guru Nanak's wife (who was left with the task of bringing up two sons after the Guru had gone on His life's mission) is lit up all the way through with the same image:

I was a shadow and am one still
I've travelled with the Sun on His course:
Have drunk of His glory
And bathed in a stream full of His light . . .
At the time I was being put through the test:
The Sun-test to which there was no end—
It was so ordained that from the darkness of the word
His rays were to take birth
And the birth pangs of them being born were to be borne,
And from the darkness of the breast
These were to be fed on the milk,
And when the Sun was to rove in all direction
And move to His journey—
The shadow was to lay with the one infant ray . . .

I remember writing again once:

Could I drink in one breath a bowl of sunshine
And give part of the Sun himself to my womb . . .

I have created characters impregnated by the sun and have gone back into the womb of eternity to trace the source of his existence. The sun touches my innermost depths. It seems that a few people like me, no matter to which country or century they belong, are in this like the Phoenicians. It is said that the phoenix is about the size of an eagle, that its plumage is crimson and gold, that it has a highly melodious voice and that only one of its species can exist at any given time. Its minimum life span is five hundred years. Some say that it is known to have lived for 1461 years but legend gives it a life of 97,200 years! When its life cycle is about to come full circle, it builds a nest of fragrant leaves and twigs and breaks into a soulful song of such passion that it is devoured by its flames. The nest is thus a veritable pyre. From the ashes arises another phoenix. And whatever remains of the ashes is offered by the new-born in worship to the Sun-temple.

Some mythologists have it that the phoenix can will the moment of its own death. In other words, when its desire for life ends, it flies straight to the Sun-temple and descends on the sacred fire. But nobody differs on one point. A new phoenix arises from the ashes of the one that is dead.

Egyptologists claim that the phoenix came from the East where the sun begins his diurnal course. Thus a historian of the ancient civilizations of the East gave its country of origin as Arabia or India—with a likelihood more of the latter country.

A Latin poet has claimed the rare bird for the crest of Roman domination; some upholders of the Christian faith weave the allegories of crucifixion and resurrection around it; and a few ingeniously interpret Virgin Mary's conception through this myth. I would only like to identify the genuine writer with the phoenix—the country and century are immaterial to me.

Scraps from a Diary

As I have said before, I have not cultivated the habit of keeping a diary. I have often tried to, but always gave up after three or four days. Sometimes I think I know the reason and then again at other times, I am not at all sure.

I was fairly young when I first attempted something like a diary. I used to put down thoughts into a little notebook and kept it carefully under lock and key. The key was concealed in a secret little corner at the back of a cupboard drawer. But I had been observed and after my marriage one day, when I was away, the cupboard was broken open and the diary discovered and scanned through. Then followed the grilling. I was asked wearisome questions about this or that little entry. After this I tore the offending things to bits and took a secret vow never again to keep a diary.

Later I thought it was a silly vow and began keeping a diary again. One day, to my dismay, I discovered the diary had been stolen from my room! It was obvious it was not the kind of thing to engage the attention of a common thief. For years I could not get over the loss . . . I am not sure I have got over it even now. I suspected it to be the work of Shanti Bibi. But even if I had wanted to, I could not have done anything about it.

I could never bring myself to write a regular diary ever again. I would of course still toy with the idea periodically— every six months or so—and would scribble a few lines. These scattered jottings I have hammered into some kind of sequential account:

I have many contemporaries,
I alone am not contemporaneous with myself

These were the first two lines of an incomplete poem, yet I knew that the expostulating with itself . . . I had not yet transferred it from that part of the heart on which it had been inscribed to paper.

A birth bereft of the 'I'
Is like a sin decorating my trayful of offerings . . .

August 22, 1968

The eyes failed to focus on the front-page coverage of the news: *Soviet Troops Occupy Czechoslovakia… Surprise Invasion to Smash Liberation Drive… Fate of Dubcek Uncertain…* My self merged into millions of strange selves… I have not suffered at the hands of fascists although I have heard and seen enough. My fallen ideals I have consequently put to social inadequacies. Not that I am unaware of the advances countries have made. The question that pains is: what has happened since?

A poem was beginning to take shape in my mind. I did not finish it. This is all that is left of it:

If a bullet is fired at me in Hanoi
And again . . . in Prague–
A sort of smoke floats in the air
The self within me aborts
And dies a premature death . . .

August 31, 1968

My Cernik said, 'Go away and urge the best brains of the country to get out while they can . . .'

Has the world only such news to offer as a present on my birthday?

To get his own horoscope made, Arthur Koestler searched for all the published papers he could find of the day he was born. He looked for every kind of information he could: which ships had been sunk, which banks had been looted, which countries had broken the terms of peace. I wrote: 'Each horoscope is a false testimony of Homo sapiens . . . it is after the broad-based pattern Koestler envisages.' What is this awful news I get therefore on my birthday?

August 6, 1968

It was well after midnight when Gulzar came on the long distance line. 'Let me duck my head first . . . You might blow me up for ringing at this hour!' I laughed, 'Who do you think I am? A Stalinist?' He joined in the laughter. 'Right-o! Then talk to a red-hot Stalinist now! Here he is squatting by my side. He egged me on to phone you . . .'

'How's Your Worship?' That was Sant Singh Sekhon's voice.

'Bearing up,' I said. 'Are you asking about my health or dictating terms of health like those of friendship to the Czechs . . .?'

'Such invasions ought not to alarm you. If the *guru* goes in disguise, the Sikh doesn't lose his faith, does he?'

'Hail the guru's five good disciples, Sekhon Sahib! After swapping one good *guru* for another, you still hold on to the same old faith! Why don't you step out of the scriptures and get down to plain words?'

Last Night

That was last night . . . the night of August 31, 1968. When this morning I invited a few Punjabi writers to meet Dr Istvan from Hungary, Sekhon was also among them. After the others left, he stayed back and wrote a poem on the recent happenings in which the prevalent Social Order abducts and rapes an innocent girl. This brings tears first to her eyes and then . . . smiles!

Such a treatment of the subject and at the hands of an 'intellectual' too, pained me deeply. To them victory was not in winning the hearts of the masses. It was in inflicting a humiliating compromise on a meek victim. What sadism.

The Czechs have this morning erased all the numbers from their houses, their streets, their markets. I wrote a poem about this silent protest, entitled *My Address:*

Today I effaced my house number and the name of the street where I live.
I wiped away the direction of every road; and still if you must search me out,
just knock at the door in each street of each city of each country.

It's curse, a benediction-both . . .
and wherever you find a free soul, that is my home!

September 7, 1968

P C Joshi had written a fine critical article on the situation. I felt like talking to him. So I sought out his telephone number and heard his candid and clear voice at the other end. He told me how unhappy Aruna Asaf Ali and his other friends were. 'Your tragedy and mine is that not only our political leaders but also our writers have pawned their brains.'

I read Gurbux Singh's article yesterday. I cannot for the life of me make out what has happened to our Punjabi writers:

To cover the nakedness of meaning
I shrouded them in words—
The words have raped the meanings today
And are ashamed to look me in the eye.

August 21, 1970

Every morning the city's different zones bark at one another . . .

Some are like dogs with owners: dogs well-looked after, with coats glossy from daily brushing, fed on bread and milk and rich chunks of meat . . .

But the great majority of them are sorry-looking specimens, gnawing away for as long as they can at a bone they have managed to salvage from the garbage heap, mangy curs with furs eaten away by fleas.

But they all bark, one louder than the other. Except for the puppies that help in and around the thatched huts of the labourers . . .

And at fall of night, the zones of the city quietly crouch down, all licking their wounds.

But come election time, they wag their tails at each other instead of snarling and growling. And a few crusts are flung at them, left-overs from the feasts.

I was born in a provincial town, Gujranwala, but the main part of my life has been lived in metropolitan cities, half in Lahore, half in Delhi; half under colonial rule, half in independent India.

But to the extent one can talk of cities as living things I knew only the skin of Lahore. Delhi was a deeper experience.

August 31, 1972

I am a chain-smoker. I love a drop of whisky too, occasionally. Indeed, I sometimes have a craving for it. But I am not an addict and I do not drink everyday. I am acutely aware of the prevailing attitudes towards a woman who smokes and drinks.

A peculiar comparison occurs to me. After all, I was born in a Sikh family. When a plate of sweet, semolina *halwa* is placed in offering before the great Sikh book *Guru Granth Sahib* the blade of a sword is passed through it. Thereupon, the simple *halwa* becomes *kraahprasad* which is distributed to congregation. Similarly, the cigarette between my fingers or the glass of drink in my hands transform themselves into something infinitely purer. The intensity of my thoughts is cut through as with the blade of a sword: and my thoughts, like the *halwa* that is transformed into *prasad,* are then ready for distribution.

April 25, 1974

The paper carries the news of Shri Ram Dhari Singh Dinkar's death. This day last week we had met at the inauguration of the Star Book fair. I was on my way out of the hall. He was ahead of me in his car and about to leave. He waved out with his hand and Davinder (who was with me) and I went across. He lowered the car window, put his hand out and seizing mine said, 'See that you don't die! The country will lose her verdure if you do . . .' I knew he had been in poor health for some time. My heart grew heavy. Yet I cheerfully replied. 'But you must stay alive to say such charming things. No one else can . . .'

Davinder's eyes grew moist. It was an agonizing question he put to me—'Didi! Why are there not such fine people writing in our language?'

Dinkarji has passed away; not only Hindi literature, but the country is much the poorer. How difficult it is to keep tears from flowing . . .

May 9, 1974

Kamleshwar, the editor of *Sarika,* has written a letter seeking
my permission to include *Mera Hutndum, Mera Dost* in
an anthology. I had written this article on Navtej Singh for
Sarika many years earlier. But what I held true at one time,
I no longer did. So I wrote immediately to Kamleshwar. I
have no companion or friend to merit a new lease of life in
printed form. Of course, I would have earned a cheque for
₹100 had I allowed the reprint, but I could not go against my
convictions . . .

One Night

How does one get so obsessed with truth from alien lands
that it becomes part of one's own being? I was reading the
Mahabharata one night when I fell asleep. I dreamt of a dove
flying in and descending on my lap. A hawk followed asking me
to release the dove that had sought my protection. The closer the
hawk drew, the tighter the dove held on to me until the hawk
demanded a piece of my flesh of equal weight instead. I readily
agreed. The alarming thing was that the dove got heavier and
heavier . . . Ultimately I had all but forfeited my life. Then the
revelation came to me . . . the dove had symbolized the pen
and the courageous resistance I had put up was against forces
trying to snatch it from my grip . . .

I woke up to find the Mahabharata open at the page in
the twelfth chapter where the Fire God goes in the guise of

a dove to Raja Usheenar for protection, but the latter prefers to give himself up to the hawk rather than give up the meek, defenceless bird.

One Day

When I had not really begun writing this autobiography I often deliberated on whether I would ever get down to anything more than the ten lines I had written and set aside . . . I have these before me as true now as they were on the day they were written:

'I am fully aware of the fact that my writings, in prose or verse, are all put together, like an illegitimate child . . .

'The crude realities of my world fell in love with my dreams and out of such an illicit union was born all that I wrote . . .

'I am aware that it would have to bear the same fate that buffets an illegitimate child . . . in other words, it would alas have to put up with the screwed-up verdict of the literary world . . .

'It is not necessary to explain what the dream was. It should indeed have been an extraordinary one to transcribe both my personal life as well as the progress of mankind, for then only could reality have risen above the human predicament. The net result, nonetheless, is that my writings have been rudely tossed about in the wind as hybrid creations.'

Thus it is that those few lines are in themselves my autobiography . . .

A Poem

I wrote *A Line in Water* in 1963. The following year when it was published, the rumour arose that the Punjab government was taking steps to ban it. Nothing of the kind happened. On the contrary, it was translated in Hindi in 1965 and in Urdu in 1966. I turned over in my mind plans to make a film script out of it. Nothing came of it because of Revti Saran Sharma's candid but well-considered advice: 'No! The novella has appeared at least a century too soon. The Indian mind is not yet ready to grasp it fully.' Basu Bhattacharya went further. 'It would be the first adult film—if at all it is screened, that is.' On re-reading it for the benefit of my friend Krishna, who undertook to translate it in English in 1974, I was overwhelmed by the character Alka as I had not been when I was writing the story . . .

When the hero tells the heroine that he pays ₹20 every time he goes to the woman who gratifies his hunger for sex, she wistfully suggests . . . 'If only I could be the one, alas! I swear by the holy truth . . .' I fell into retrospection. Imroz had been retelling some difficult moments of his life to me, one of which was as illustrated in the novella. It had produced from me the same reaction in exactly the same words.

I recognized my own self then. Only Amrita could have said what Alka said. No other woman could have had the courage . . .

Although a writer has a deep kinship with each of the characters he creates, there is still a certain distance. With Alka, I discovered complete identification. So much so that that very night (September 7, 1964) I wrote a poem addressed to her:

More than a thousand keys had I—
One for each entrance door . . .
Beyond which, some possibly had parlours
And some had bedrooms wrapped up in heavy curtains.
The anxieties of the owners were mine sometimes
Like the pain in the breast—
Pain—that when I woke up, would wake up with me,
And stream off into my dreams at night . . .'
But ever ahead of my steps
Was the Ramayanic line of honour
That I daren't go past . . .
And I gave back the tears to whom they belonged
And withdrew from the line . . .
Look! I did indeed have as many keys
As I had stories and characters!

But what magic was in the key to your house
That when I opened the lock to your door
I saw the line of honour was not before my feet
But behind . . .
And there in front—you were not there . . . but I . . .

This incidentally, is the only poem I have ever written under the inspiration of my own creation . . .

A Porch

I vividly see the furrowed forehead of my father even from this point of time. He seems always to be looking on sternly as I go through life.

My first book was published early in 1936. For this achievement the Maharaja of Kapurthala sent me a gift of ₹200 with his love and blessings. A few days later, the Maharani of Nabha (who was at one time a pupil of Father) sent me a *sari*. The postman knocked at our door the third time. Visions of another money order or parcel flashed across my mind and as I hastened to run to the door, I was stopped in my tracks by the stern look from Father.

I did not at that time quite understand why there was this rebuke in my father's eyes and what he expected of me. But I do remember that I was rather deflated, and I vaguely felt that it was unbecoming of me to show such eagerness. I would understand all this a little better later in life.

Another Night

It was on the night of the wedding ceremony forty years ago. I went up to the terrace and wept my heart out in the pitch-black dark. Father knew about my state of mind and he followed me. I kept on telling him again and again, 'I do not want to be married.'

The bridegroom and his party had already arrived. They had finished their dinner when Father received a message—should anyone ask, he was to say that he was giving so many thousands of rupees as part of the dowry.

Both Father and I had given prolonged thought to this wedding. All went on satisfactorily until this message was sprung upon us. Not having so much hard cash, he was stung to the quick. When he told me of this move from their side, my one and only thought was to put myself to death then and there . . .

The night was oppressive with anxiety. A friend of Mother smelt something untoward in the air. The honour of the bride and her family was at stake. Briskly, but quietly, she stole away from the din and clatter, removed all the gold bangles she had on her hands and returning with the same speed, placed them before Father. He broke down. To me this scene was worse than death . . .

The truth came to us dramatically. No cash had been demanded. The fuss had been engineered on purpose to seal the lips of widemouthed relatives. But the entire sequence had left an indelible mark on me. All was right with my world if that friend of my mother could unhesitatingly give all she had in the name of friendship and honour. Faith can be shattered; but just one step away from as far as thought can reach is trust, and trust is what truly sustains hope in the world . . .

One Word More

When I read *Greek Passion* a long time ago, the case of the shepherd boy fascinated me. Having been cast for the role of Christ, he undergoes spiritual exercises that he thinks will discipline him for complete identification with the part. He succeeds to a degree that evokes the antagonism of the entire village. He fights against wrong and injustice and provokes the villagers to the point of stoning him to death. There is one man in the village who has grasped the truth of his character. He takes him atop a hill for burial. 'His name is inscribed in the snows of today that will melt tomorrow and course it down the streams and rivers . . .'

I could well say as much for myself. Whatever I had in me has been buried under the snows . . . that will course down streams and rivers when the snows melt. Then will come into the world those who will have faith in the word they write with new pens . . . and in the intensity of the ideas that move their pens they will reappear in that part of me that is being buried in the silence of the snows.

From Reality to Reality

An autobiography is generally taken to be the gospel truth set in glittering words of gold . . . an artifact of self-praise. The basic truth is the writer's own need. This is a continuous process that leads from one reality to another.

There is an indefinable something that is seen without effort; there is something else that is revealed only when you look for it. In search of that, the dust that overlays thought has to be put through a sieve. What is thus sought and obtained is also an aspect of reality.

All art consists of re-creating what was created before. This process also is reality. Truth put into the crucible of the womb must give birth to truth. The effort to get down to the bottom of one reality is itself to reach out to yet another.

The common reader of fiction recognizes the characters he comes across from the emotional experiences they go through. As against the myriad of fictional characters, the writer of the autobiography attracts concentrated attention. The reader and the writer are face to face. The writer of the autobiography invites the reader to his house beyond the threshold of normal constraint. And compromise with the truth is an insult . . . not to the one invited, but to the one extending the invitation.

There are two types of writers: those who are writers first and last and those who are content to play with writing. Nothing less than the truth as they see it is acceptable to those who are writers first and last.

The Battle is On

This script I am writing for the film Basu Bhattacharya is making on Indira Gandhi is sheer joy. I am always present when the shooting is done. It has given me an insight into Indiraji's charming, enigmatic personality. Certainly things get said that have absolutely nothing to do with the film but have their own meaning. To the extent I can, my effort is to write about them eventually. To cite one instance: before he started shooting one day, Basu Da observed some specks of dust on the portraits of Motilal and Jawaharlal Nehru hanging on the wall. 'Will you please flick these off with a corner of your *sari palloo*?' he suggested. The obvious symbolic significance was that he thus wanted to show the prevalent congestions and confusions in the country's situation being cleared. But Indiraji flatly refused to do anything of the kind:

With a duster—yes! Not with any part of my sari. No matter whose portraits they are I cannot be demonstrative . . . or sentimental that way. Were I to use my sari, I'd promptly have to go and change . . . I certainly have no love or respect for dust!

That is as it should be. Then the film must show her as she is. Of course, Basu Da ultimately shot Indiraji using the duster. Such an aspect of her individuality cannot be seen in the film, nor can the atmosphere created be caught by the camera.

At one of our sessions, I posed the not uncommon question: 'Indiraji! Has the fact of your being a woman created any specific difficulties in your working with others?' Her reply was immediate:

Well, something perhaps can be said on both sides . . . not that I've ever given much thought to it . . . I've always taken myself to be a human being, and I had all along known that I was capable of doing anything men can do. I've found, in fact, that I can grapple with any situation better than men. Physically I would not presume to match a man's strength . . . but in every other way I am confident I am more capable . . . That's why perhaps I've never considered the accidental factor of being a woman as a handicap. Those who had taken me merely for a woman, had certainly underestimated me. But that was how their minds worked . . . not mine. I am aware of plenty of loose talk—some of it of course reaches my ears . . . not that I set much store by such things.

What comes with natural ease in her does not to me. The path ahead of me was indeed steep and tortuous. True, I have overcome a lot of difficulties—but my battle is still on . . . I have headed these pages with Indiraji's endless political struggles in my mind. In the present context, it has a bearing on my personal life . . . which is relatively of much less importance.

This relates to the time I was still at Patel Nagar, living in a house without electricity and working at the Radio Station. The neighbours had a battery-operated radio set, from which my little children had the satisfaction of hearing my voice every evening. On my return one night, my son insisted on a promise from me. 'Promise me Mamma! Promise me you won't speak on Bholoo's radio!' This was a sequel to the little quarrel he had with his friend next door to whose house he did not want to go any more . . . So why should my voice . . .

Such prattle, amusing at the time, provokes a wishful thought. If only I could keep my books away from the hands of those who will only throw stones at them . . .

The advice of my friends is that I should have this book published in all languages except Punjabi. I cannot accept this because serious readers would hold it against me . . . I too cannot bring myself to break away from them and from the language that is my first love . . .

I am ready, therefore, to pay the price . . .

6

ON ONE PALM HENNA
—ON THE OTHER BLISTERS

This book, *The Revenue Stamp*, was printed in 1976 in Punjabi. In 1977 the Hindi and English versions were published. On 3rd September a reader had sent me a newspaper clipping, which contained a protest to the Punjab government to ban this book. This case dragged on for months. I had no idea about who handled this file but what I came to know from a reliable source was that the complaint was made at the instigation of one my contemporaries, who made them raise this question that the book was hurting religious sentiments.

I breathed for many months the air that was filled with sparks but then the time came when the fireball vanished into the air.

And to offset the earlier tension, I received a letter from Indiraji dated 11 April 1979, regarding this book.

12 Willingdon Crescent
New Delhi - 110011
11th April 1979

Dear Amritaji,

It needed quite a search before I could locate your book—Maneka had borrowed it—and I read it at one go that same night. It is moving, not for what it says but because of the sensitivity which comes through so vividly. It is *you* and yet there is something universal. Patterns are different but the essence of dreams and of struggles exist in some measure in all humans. Most people bury their real selves in some unfathomable depth of their being and just skim the surface of life. It is the privilege of the artist and the poet to be more poignantly aware.

Yours sincerely
Indira Gandhi

P.S.

I scribbled this on the flight from Delhi to Jammu but it could be typed on my return this evening.

This book was published in Gujarati in 1980. It became a course book in SNDT Women's University of Bombay and was prescribed for two years as classic literature.

In 1980

I was not feeling well, so when I went to Bulgaria, it was suggested that I have treatment with mineral water in a sanatorium there for ten days. When I had all the medical check-ups done, the doctors diagnosed that I had some heart problem. At that moment the simple me fell in love with my heart. I remember the day, it was the sixth of October. I wrote two poems, one on the same night and the other the next night The first poem was—

A Complaint

Oh deceitful! You my beloved.
You rule the breath, so how come you are tired?
The masses can rebel but should you?
Oh deceitful! You my beloved.
At the first hint of death you got scared,
While I on your name have passed my whole life
hearing the complaints of the world.
Oh deceitful! You my beloved.
What could be the fate of that tree;
the fault of the branch,
To have fallen in love with a bird like you,
Oh deceitful! You my beloved,
I don't insist on my world; if you want
to yours I'll go.
I love you, through the deserts of death
you I'll follow,
Oh deceitful! You my beloved.

And the other poem was the *Processing*

I have come on a pilgrim to the river of my soul,
I offer the sun in obeisance.

Churning this very river, this sun, I got
And ever since, on my forehead the sun,
I placed with care.
Its my love for the sun that I give it
away to the world.

I have come on a pilgrim to the river of my soul,
I give the sun in obeisance.

I ask the river for a little water—to
wash the hands of the world.
So I could place the sun in the hands
And say—go distribute the light everywhere
I have come on a pilgrim to the river of my soul,
I give the sun in obeisance.

On a pilgrimage to the river I have come,
To sprinkle my ashes, in my own river.
Oh god! to what an enlightenment my madness
has brought me;

I have come on a pilgrim to the river of my soul,
I offer the sun in obeisance.

A Blank Sheet

On October 18, I returned from Bulgaria. And on October 26 in
the early hours of the morning at 2 o'clock I received a phone

call from Bombay saying that Sahir was no more-he had died of heart attack.

This was the night which turned to the night of twenty days earlier, when in Bulgaria, the doctors had told me about my heart problem. And it was the night I had written the poem and saw myself sprinkling my ashes, in my own river.

Suddenly I looked at my hands, these very hands had scattered away my ashes; how did it happen that instead of my ashes they turned into Sahir's? This mistake was of death or of my hands?

It reminded me of the day when the first Asian Writers Conference was held in 1956. Every writer and poet was given identification tag which everyone pinned on one's coat. Sahir had taken off his tag and pinned it on my own and taking my tag put it on his coat. Noting this somebody pointed out that we were wearing the wrong tags. Sahir had laughed and said maybe the person who gave them the tags had made the mistake. We neither tried nor we wanted to try to correct the mistake. And after many years when I heard Sahir was no more that I felt that death had read that tag, the one in my name, pinned on Sahir's coat and had taken the decision.

No words came between our friendship. It was a beautiful relationship in silence. When the book containing the poems I had written on his love got the Akademi award, the press photographer wanted a photograph of me writing on paper. When they had gone away, I observed the paper and to my astonishment found that I had written only one word, Sahir, over and over again. I hadn't written it consciously but observing my madness I became conscious.

Soon, I was filled with anxiety at what a fateful day it would be when my photograph scribbling his name would be in the morning newspaper.

The fateful day never came. The picture was published but the paper in my hand seemed blank.

It was another thing that with regret and remorse I saw the photograph. Why did the paper in my hand seem blank when it wasn't so?

The dignity of a blank paper is even there today. I knew that Sahir did read this book which contained my love for him but after that neither I nor he ever mentioned this book.

I remember that once in a symposium of Urdu Poetry, when the programme had ended, many people went to Sahir to ask for his autograph. When I was the only one left I smilingly extended my hand like a blank piece of paper and he wrote his name saying, 'On this blank cheque I have signed. Whatever the amount you want, fill it in and get it cashed.' I knew it was the skin of palm that was fated to be an empty paper for no words could be written on it.

Even today there are no words. In this book whatever that has been written, even today in 1980, it is the tale of an empty blank paper.

The beginning of this tale was silence and the intensity of it too was carried out in silence.

Forty years ago when Sahir used to come to see me in the Lahore days, he would come, silently smoke cigarettes and leave when the ashtray was brimming with cigarette butts.

And I would, after he was gone, light those cigarette butts. Our smoke mingled in the air as did our breath, the words of our poems too.

I am thinking that the air can cover any space. Earlier it used to cover the distance of our two cities, and today I am sure that it would be covering the space between this world and that world.

In 1983

This year too like the earlier put henna on my one palm, while the other writhed in pain from the blisters given by it.

In 1982 Bhartiya Jnanpith had selected my book of poems *Kagaz Te Canvas* for the award. My son who was averse to marry again after his divorce, reversed his decision. At the end of the year he married a girl, very gentle in nature.

When 1983 started Jabalpur University honoured me with a D.Lit. degree. And it was the seventh of May, when I received a lawyer's notice. I was aghast, the notice pertained to my book of poems, which was recently awarded. The objections were about the poems regarding the nine dreams of Guru Nanak's mother, before the birth of Guru Nanak, in which I had hurt the religious sentiments and hence a criminal case would be filed against me.

No one must have experienced, as I did, the power of press, one that was pro and the other anti. The poem on which the issue was raised, was published in 1969. And now, after 14 years, the book which received the Jnanpith Award, containing that poem was being considered objectionable. Many writers and newspapers had raised their voice in defence of the poem. This issue ultimately reached Longowal. The issuing of the notice was not in his knowledge. Without disclosing his identity, he gave a long interview in the Punjab edition of *Indian Express*, from which I came to know that a Punjabi newspaper had written many provoking articles for quite a few months. He said that some people who were jealous of Amrita Pritam used the name of the religious institution to further their own goals.

Those days, how tense they were for me. The incident came to an end. I would like to quote from my diary published in 1984.

> *It was the night of 14th May. In an half awakened, half asleep state, like a cry, the words came out 'My Nanak, I have always imagined you but today I want to see you, the actual you—not from the figment of imagination but by these eyes of flesh and blood.' How shrill the cry was I don't know but suddenly in front of my eyes a glow appeared and an electric current passed through me. No face appeared but I heard a very distinct voice. 'Have you seen the proof you wanted?' And in the half awakened state I said, 'Yes, I have seen it.'*

And it was the same 1983, when my granddaughter Shilpi was born. On December 16 at Vishwa Bharti I received from Indiraji the D.Lit. degree.

In 1984

This year from the point of view of my personal life and the fate of the country came as if a glass bangle had broken on the arm of culture, as if a pearl had fallen out from the ring of history.

Here I would like to quote a few paragraphs from my diary of 1984.

A Few Pages From My Diary

About a month back, on 20th September, there was a call from the Prime Minister's House asking me to go there at 6.45 p.m.

That evening I spent more than an hour with Indiraji. She asked me how Indianization of our time could be possible as suggested by Shri Kailash Patiji. I told her that this could be properly answered by our scientists; I could only speak of the spiritual importance of new Indianized timings. But I was more worried about the forecast of an impending danger to her person.

'It is not danger only to my person, but to the whole country,' she said, and remarked that great weaknesses had crept into our intelligence. Our laws were so much complicated and had so many loopholes that no right step at right time could be taken unhindered. Everything was lost in words. A word here and there on paper could upset the whole thing. The judiciary, the administration too, come up for comment along with security. She was upset and remarked, 'I see darkness around.'

And now when the light of the country is gone—O God, who is there to listen to me, that the blot is on the conscience of our own people, and we are engulfed by darkness.

31 October 1984
11.30 p.m.

It was 3 o'clock and still dark. I was not fully asleep, when all of a sudden there was light like dawn. This light kept rising and merging in the sky.

Then this light became stationary, out of which Indiraji's calm smiling face emerged.

I cannot describe this experience in words. Her face was becoming one with light, but still it was prominent.

Then my eyes fell on the earth. There were several animals of the same height and structure. As if they were animals of the same species. They were looking around with wide open eyes.

I visualized in them anti-national forces conspiring. They were sitting like a group of conspirators.

This sight remained before me for quite some time, was afraid that I would not be able to pin-point them in life because they were all alike. I was not able to understand their language. But their looks spoke of some hidden conspiracy which said that our country was in danger.

2 November 1984
Past midnight

On the morning of 31st October, when she was shot by her own guards, what a shock she might have got? The words she uttered were: 'What are you doing?'

What kind of faith she had reposed in the goodness of human beings that even when her body was riddled by bullets she could say 'What are you doing?'

We can understand the pang. But incidents of loot and arson cannot be understood.

The people who dare commit such crimes are turning a deaf ear to the very person who is again saying 'What are you doing?'

I think whenever any wrong will be committed by anyone in this country, if one has the power of hearing, one will be able to listen to her voice saying, 'What are you doing?'

Indiraji is not the name of an individual, but it is the name of the conscience of this land, all lands.

2 November 1984
Evening

Who knows the secret of cosmic powers? I don't know how some waves of the imagination get in touch with those powers, or the threads of these powers come into contact with our mind; and become the spectators of ethereal dreams.

Last night I saw a thick forest in my dream. Under the shade of a tree. I saw a *rishi* in trance. A divine woman, more like a fairy comes there. She leaves a year-old girl in front of the rishi. Them *rishi* is still in trance. The child starts playing with flowers and leaves. There is no one else around. But I hear a voice saying to me: 'The Indira you have known in the present is the re-birth of the same of ancient times. She was born on this earth by an earthly saint and mother who was a divine woman.'

I keep looking at the child absorbed in playing with flowers and leaves of the forest. I want to see in this child a resemblance to the person I know—when I wake up.

6 November 1984

A realization dawned on me that Kailash Patiji mentioned only that ruler has a right to start a new calendar who takes upon himself all the miseries and debts of his people. Such a person attains the position of a person beyond death. Kailash Patiji suggested to Indiraji that this was not the time to start a new calendar, but he added: 'If you Indianize our time you will attain that calibre.'

These are the two recognized procedures to be beyond death. I have strange feeling that Indiraji has adopted the third path by taking upon herself the violence of her people and has gone beyond death which is termed as *'Kaalijayee'*.

Whether we unfortunate people know it or not, but she has become *'Kaalijayee'*.

7 November 1984

Today I have been reading a hand-written letter which Indiraji wrote in reply to a complaint of mine. While talking to her I had said, 'Why did you not come to the Bhartiya Jnanpith function? For me, more than the award itself, the award from your hand mattered.'

She replied to me in words and action. She presented to me the D.Litt. degree of Viswa Bharati in December 1983. Before that she wrote me a letter, dated 17 May 1983:

Dear Amrita,

The other day you came to see me. I felt very bad that I had not accepted the Jnanpith's request to give away this award. I did not think you would mind. How can I make up for this delay? You know or should know that you are one of my favourite persons, even though I have read a very small portion of your poetry. Apart from the beauty of thoughts and words, you have courage and that in my view is the basic virtue, for how can one be true to oneself or to any idea without it?

With fond wishes,

Sincerely,

Indira.

I know I have the strength to be true to myself, but there is also a deep-rooted sadness which envelops me by untoward happenings around me. I have passed through this experience many a time. While facing the difficulties I have thought about Indiraji's courage. I was desperate today. To gain strength I read her letter several times.

When someone picks up a weapon, the first wound he inflicts is not on a human being, but on humanity. The first drop of blood shed is not of a human being but of humanity, and dead bodies lying on the roads are not human beings, but humanity.

18 November 1984

It is the birthday of Indiraji. For me birth is reality, death is like a sound of water going away from the water.

Whom to tell that Indiraji is not the name of a person, that it is the name of the conscience of our land?

I feel like saying this on her behalf:

I am the ray of light, reflecting in the vast
waters of the world.
No one can touch the body of light.
The paths mean nothing to me.
You name the path, I will walk on it.
This is the journey of the flow of light.
If you wish, I shall be there.
Paths mean nothing to me.

19 November 1984

A television team from the BBC recorded a programme, and talking about Indiraji, I explained the music of cosmic powers as scientific reality, and said, 'The day when Indiraji was born, we don't know which ray of light and which cosmic music was engraved in her mind. But we know that this phenomenon gave birth to a vision of United India in her. And this was the vision she wanted all her people to share with her.'

The night of the 27th—when I was asleep I heard some divine music and also heard a voice: 'You talk about the music of cosmic powers, but you have never listened to this music. Now listen to it.'

I saw a circle of light spreading across the whole sky revolving in a circle, constituted of small particles of light with music emerging from them.

Spell-bound I listen to this music. There is no one else in front of this circle. I feel as if I were also in the sky and the only witness of this sight. Someone tells me, 'This is the moment you talked about, and here is the music when Indiraji was born.'

Then the scene changes with the change in music. The circle of light changes into a circle of fire along with sounds of explosions. But all these sounds have a unique rhythm. This continuation of sounds and music captivates me when I again hear the same voice: 'This is the same cosmic sound of music and sight of the moment when Indiraji was shot at.'

All this changes itself into a vast sea, on the shore of which I am standing, looking at the sky, trying to listen to the cosmic music. The sound is receding in the distance; it is difficult to tell whether it is the sound of music or the sound of explosions.

I stood for a while on the seashore. The fading lights of evening turn into deep darkness, a vast expanse of darkness.

Now I withdraw from the seashore and start climbing up a road which leads to the parapet of a fort. Here I find hundreds of stairs going down. In the middle of these stairs I find her standing as she has come out from the room at the right. Seeing her, the tears well up in my eyes. I cannot utter a word. She looks at me and says, 'Look, you are not to weep. You are to write about the cosmic music you have just heard and the sight you have just witnessed.'

Still I want to say something to her but she disappears. There is no one in the stairs, they are empty, they are going down into the darkness.

27-28 November 1984
1.30 a.m.

Time has compelled this me of flesh and blood to pass through the rigours of life but that pain has done the kindness that my soul has had glimpses of that stage which can be called beyond time and space.

In this world full of hatred, the time that is left to learn, I feel if only I could see it as an onlooker. And with a cool mind be an alibi to the agony and ecstasy I am going through. That is why even to play with my two grandchildren is giving me satisfaction, while I put forth my inner experiences on paper.

Whatever I have experienced through my dreams, those details are too long to tell. Perhaps I'll be able to expound all that in a separate book. All these writings of mine are a relationship of the 'red thread'. A sect of Zenism, who had recognized psychic relationship with the supreme power, called themselves the 'Red Thread Zens'. Likewise I too want to call my new experiences a relationship of the Red Thread.

In May 1986, I was nominated to the Rajya Sabha, which has widened the scope of opportunities to express my thinking. But there are many things whose expression hasn't come to my lips. I am thankful to the AIR archives who have preserved a major part in my own words which after my death would be the last page of this book.